Richard-Michael Diedrich

The Dragon Has Many Faces

Conceptualizations of Rural Communities in North Wales
and the Development of "Anthropology at Home" in Britain

Interethnische Beziehungen und Kulturwandel

Ethnologische Beiträge zu soziokultureller Dynamik

hreausgegeben von

Prof. Dr. Jürgen Jensen, Universtät Hamburg

Band 4

LIT

Richard-Michael Diedrich

The Dragon Has Many Faces

Conceptualizations of Rural Communities in North Wales and the Development of "Anthropology at Home" in Britain

LIT

Cip-Kurztitelaufnahme der Deutschen Bibliothek

Diedrich, Richard-Michael
The Dragon Has Many Faces:
Conceptualizations of Rural Communities in North Wales and the Development of "Anthropology at Home" in Britain / Richard-Michael Diedrich. – Münster ; Hamburg : Lit 1993
   (Interethnische Beziehungen und Kulturwandel; Bd. 4.)
   ISBN 3-89473-646-1

NE: GT

© LIT VERLAG   Dieckstr. 73   48145 Münster   Tel. 0251-235091
                    Hallerplatz 5   20146 Hamburg   Tel. 040-446446

There is a theory which states that if ever anyone discovers exactly what the Universe is for and why it is here, it will instantly disappear and be replaced by something even more bizarre and inexplicable.

There is another theory which states that this has already happened.

Douglas Adams • The Restaurant at the End of the Universe • Pan Books, London 1980.

Contents

PREFACE 1
1 INTRODUCTION
   The divided kingdom 5
2 THEORIES OF COMMUNITY
   Communities as wholes, microcosms and types 11
3 VOYAGE INTO THE BLACK (W)HOLE
   The social anthropology of Britain in the 1950s
   and 1960s 27
4 THE REVIVAL OF COMMUNITY STUDIES 35
5 CULTURE, SYMBOLISM AND COMMUNITY 42
6 COMMUNITY STUDIES IN THE 1980s
   Towards a new social anthropology of Britain? 56
7 THE DRAGON HAS MANY FACES
   Economy and society in Wales 74
8 COFIA TRYWERYN!
   The anthropology of rural communities in Wales
   and the discourse of Welshness 86
9 STRANGERS AND PARTISANS
   English anthropologists in North Wales 116
CONCLUSION
   An "almost tribal thing": community and identity
   in North Wales 149
BIBLIOGRAPHY 160
INDEX 170

PREFACE

This book is based on my M.A. thesis which was submitted to the University of Hamburg in 1992. Naturally, I now see the original text in a different, rather more critical light, however, I still believe that the text is a critical contribution to the understanding of Welsh communities.

The original idea for the M.A. thesis stemmed from my personal interest in the cultures of Wales. I have been familiar with the Porthmadog area in the northern county of Gwynedd for thirteen years. However, my outlook has changed considerably during those years. Every time I came to the area I stayed with a local Welsh-English family in the small village of Minffordd and their kind hospitality has contributed much to my feeling of emotional attachment to this part of Wales. In 1989 I came to Wales for an entirely different reason and as part of a group of students from the Department of Anthropology of the University of Hamburg. The data which will be used to substantiate some of my arguments were taken from informal interviews that a fellow student, Helge Ludwig, and myself conducted during one month of fieldwork in the Porthmadog/Blaenau Ffestiniog area. Being aware that the short period of fieldwork would seriously limit the opportunity for participant observation, we decided to do as many informal interviews as we could. All, except one, of the fourteen interviews took place in the home of the informants and most lasted several hours — our main informants (four couples: three middle class and one working class couple) were interviewed twice. The aim of our fieldwork was to gain insights into the conceptualization of Welsh identity. Since this practical exercise in field research was limited to a period of one month, due to the limited financial support by the University of Hamburg, we thought that it might be a good idea to interview ethnically mixed couples because we believed that ethnic identity might be more pronounced in a mixed ethnic environment. All informants showed great interest in our research. The questions we put to our informants about their perceptions of their own ethnic identity were freely answered. A substantial amount of information, which we could not have gathered in a different setting, was gained from the discussions within the families. The English partner tended to question the Welsh partner's perception of his/her identity which revealed much about the relationship, in ethnic terms, and provided us with addition insight in the problem of interethnic relationships on the micro-level. Our informants took a lively interest in our fieldwork and their contribution to our understanding of Welsh culture has made this book possible. In this sense, this book is also the fulfillment of an obligation towards all those people who took such a remarkable interest in our fieldwork, thus making it a thoroughly rewarding experience. The book is dedicated to them.

There are a number of people I wish to thank. To my friend and colleague Helge Ludwig I am indebted for his invaluable contribution to our fieldwork and for his lively interest and good talk over the past few years. I am particularly grateful to Prof. Rolf Wirsing whose friendship and advice encouraged me to continue studying social anthropology. The constructively critical comments of Prof. A. P. Cohen, Edinburgh, on my M.A. thesis have been a major inspiration for the rewriting of the original thesis. I also have to express my gratitude to Prof. Jürgen Jensen for giving me the opportunity to publish this book, and Prof. M. K. H. Eggert, my teacher during my formative undergraduate years in archaeology, whose critical comments often brought me "down to earth" again.

I wish to thank David Matthews, who did the proof reading of the manuscript — his patience in enduring the social scientists' "gibberish" was remarkable — and, last but not least, Maren Diedrich, Wolfram Latsch and my parents.

My debt to Kerstin Römhildt cannot be expressed in words.

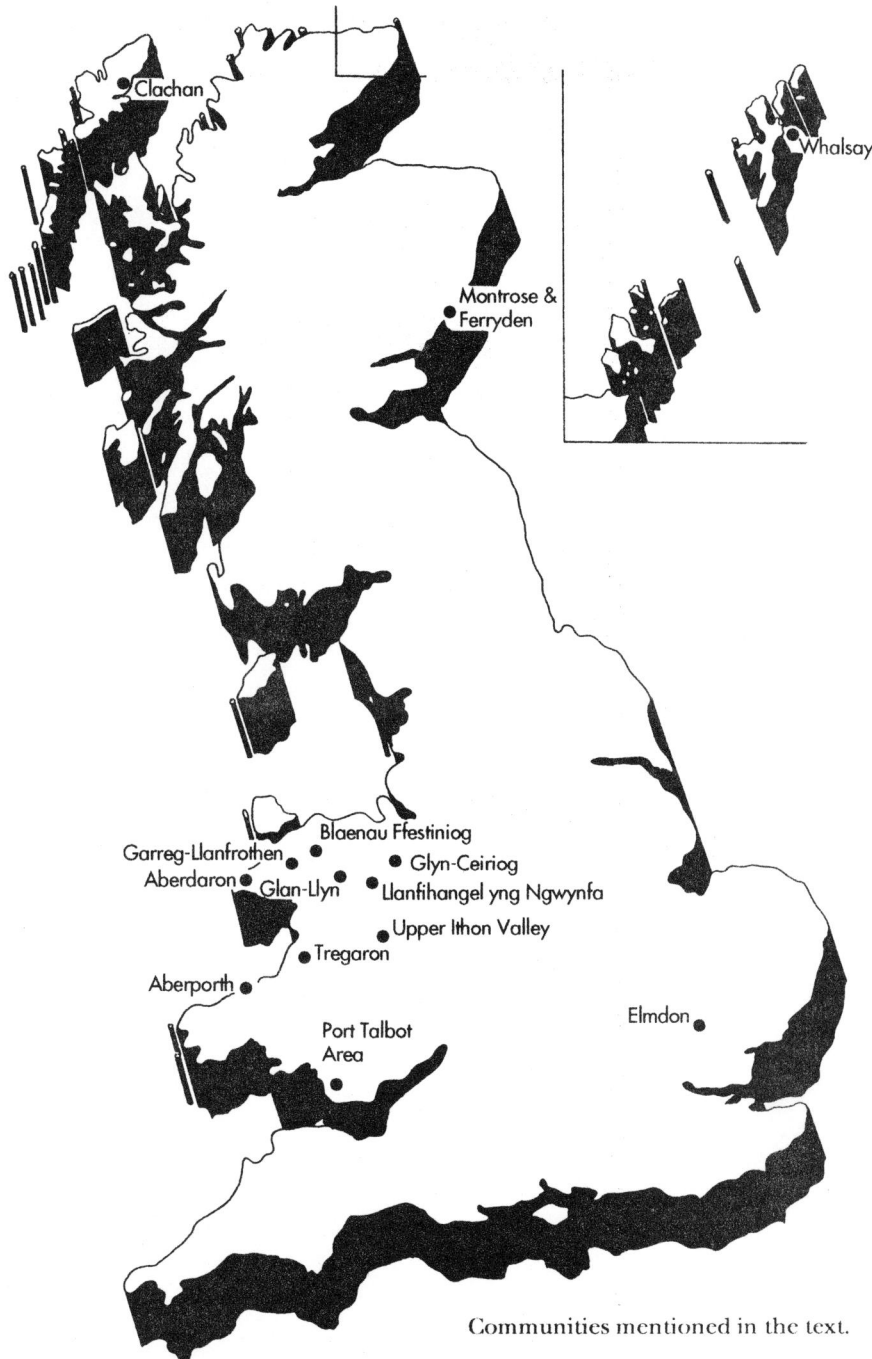

Communities mentioned in the text.

1 INTRODUCTION

THE DIVIDED KINGDOM

The growing tensions between the centre and the "Celtic Fringe" have been a prominent theme of the work of many sociologists and social anthropologists since the mid-1970s. Michael Hechter's (1975) book "Internal Colonialism" and Tom Nairn's (1982) "The Break-Up of Britain", first published in 1976, have been important contributions to the deconstruction of the myth of a homogeneous British culture, and when anthropologists revived the research into the rural communities in the British Isles, they emphasized the diversity and cultural distinctiveness of its local cultures. The revival of community studies in the 1970s was to a great extent caused by a growing awareness of the rapidly increasing pace of social change within the anthropologists' own society. It was also the continuation of a discourse on the state of human society which had found its most profound expression during a time in which European societies were deeply changed.

The idea of community has exerted a remarkable hold over the intellectual mind for at least the last hundred years. During the nineteenth century the Industrial Revolution radically changed the face of European societies. The changes which were part of the process of industrialization affected every aspect of life. This process, states Evans (1983:101), "... represents the most profound and thoroughgoing change yet experienced by mankind in society." It is not surprising that the intellectuals which were concerned with the understanding of human societies took up the challenge and tried to gain insights into the nature of the process. Change was explained in terms of evolutionary theories which became fashionable after the success of Darwin's "The Origin of Species", first published in 1859[1]. But the success of Darwin's theory stimulated a very un-Darwinian

---

1   Darwin's success strengthened the older evolutionary theories which were inspired by the writers of the Enlightenment: "There were obvious continuities with writers of the

evolutionary theory of human history. Kuper (1988:2-3) thinks that: "Perhaps the main difficulty with Darwin's theory was his idea that evolution did not imply direction or progress, that it did not follow any plan." The evolutionists "... were much more likely to believe with Spencer that human history was a history of progress, and that all living societies could be ranked on a single evolutionary scale." The process of change they experienced in their own societies was, therefore, basically conceptualized as the historically determined movement of society from one type of social organization to another: Marx and Engels saw capitalist society developing out of feudalism (Marx & Engels [1848]1971, Engels [1883] 1978), Durkheim believed in a change in the form of social solidarity from mechanical to organic solidarity (Durkheim [1893]1977), and Tönnies envisioned the decline of *Gemeinschaft* or community, and the rise of *Gesellschaft* or society (Tönnies [1887]1979). Each was "... acutely sensitive to living in the ruins of an old social order amid the envisioned outlines of a new one beyond the horizon." (Gusfield 1975:3) They were convinced that the traditional forms of social organization which had prevailed in Europe for so long would inevitably be replaced by a new form of social organization. The *new order* was conceptualized in contrast to the old "traditional society" behind which they discerned a primeval or primitive society. "The anthropologists took this primitive society as their special subject, but in practise primitive society proved to be their own society (as they understood it) seen in a distorting mirror ... . Like their most reflective contemporaries, in short, the pioneer anthropologists believed that their own was an age of massive transition. They looked back in order to understand the nature of the present, on the assumption that modern society had evolved from its antithesis." (Kuper 1988:5) But for the time being the "primitive society" was to be found elsewhere.

The interpretation of human associations in terms of a dichotomy — community-society, mechanical solidarity-organic solidarity, primitive/traditional-civilized/modern — is the fundamental prerequisite of most community studies (at least, those which were done until the 1960s). It was mainly influenced by the theories of Tönnies and Durkheim. However their understanding of the changes of society was coloured by their respective ideal-models of human association and sometimes even by

---

Scottish and French Enlightenment, and more immediately with Herbert Spencer and the Utilitarians in England and with Comte and the Positivists in France." (Kuper 1988:3)

nostalgia for the old and a disgust for the new order; the "loss of community was *the* lamentable fact of their period in history." (Gusfield 1975:5, emphasis added) Norbert Elias (1974:xiii) sees the lamenting of the loss of community, and especially the development of Tönnies' ideas about *Gemeinschaft* and *Gesellschaft*, as a result of a loss of confidence in the present and the future and a return to an idealized past by the middle class: "The feeling that industry, science and urban life were a kind of Pandora's box, a source of evil, gained ascendancy over the belief in progress." Marx, however, did not lament the *loss of community*: "As an heir to the enlightenment belief in progress through science, Marx saw much value in a capitalism that had destroyed the 'idiocy of rural life'." (Gusfield 1975:6) Capitalism, he thought, would free the individual from the limiting, coercive and demoralizing way of life of the traditional (feudal) society.

The concept of a *Gemeinschaft/Gesellschaft* dichotomy was thus the result of the scepticism with which many social thinkers of the time viewed the process of change caused by the industrial revolution. For Tönnies ([1887]1979) *Gemeinschaft* and *Gesellschaft*, and for Durkheim ([1893]1977; [1897]1966) mechanical solidarity and organic solidarity, primarily characterized the quality of human relationships. *Gemeinschaft*, and its fragmentary survival in the rural communities, was described, with a certain romanticism, as an organic whole within which, the people had the opportunity to express their personalities freely and creatively, the human relationships were intimate and enduring, and the people united in mutual understanding. Urban, industrial society, *Gesellschaft*, was used to characterize the opposite state of human relationships. Estrangement of the individual — from his labour, from his fellow human beings, from his own personality, etc. — is the basic characteristic of *Gesellschaft*. Within modern industrial society the individual was seen to be isolated and defined by external determinants — entangled in a net of contractual ties over which the individual had almost no power.

The typology derived from the works of Durkheim, Tönnies, etc. is, Bell and Newby (1971:25) claim, "... the most relevant theoretical inheritance for modern community studies ...". But of all those nineteenth century theorists, Durkheim is by far the most important for British social anthropology. It was his positivism that helped to consolidate the anthropological functionalism in Britain (Boon 1982:54). The community-society dichotomy survived as a part of the functionalist or structural-functionalist theories and was the most important concept for the anthropological study of community in the British Isles until the mid 1960s.

An explicit criticism of modern industrial society is a prominent feature of community studies. This is not surprising, since rural communities in modern industrialized societies were and still are subject to severe pressures of change imposed by an urban-centred society. Furthermore, I believe that the criticism of modern industrial society is, in a way, also closely connected to the individual's choice to take up anthropology as a subject. Anthony Jackson (1987:8) has characterized the difference between anthropologists and sociologists, basically as the difference between people who have distaste for, and people who have a love for, modern society. He argued that anthropologists tried to escape modern society in imagination, if not in fact: "In essence, anthropologists are the folklorists of the exotic." (Ibid.) However, I believe that this rather unkind characterization of anthropologists can tell only part of the story. I will argue that the focus on differences within one's own society is a kind of political action — especially in a society, such as British society, which emphasizes the cultural homogeneity of the nation-state (the *United* Kingdom). An important motivation for doing anthropological research into rural communities in the British Isles is, I believe, the anthropologist's concern with the quality of life in the society in which he/she lives (cf. Gusfield 1975: chapter 4). The study of the "other" — the urban based anthropologist studying rural communities — is also a search for "political" alternatives to a society which he/she conceives as alienating, bureaucratic, unjust and exploiting. Obviously, such a search for other life styles in order to learn something which could change one's own society bears the risk of idealization of the "other". The native anthropologist is subject to a different phenomenon of idealization, especially when his culture is threatened by powerful forces emanating from an alien centre. Such an idealization is evident in the studies of rural Welsh communities by the Welsh social geographers from the University College of Wales at Aberystwyth in the 1950s. Their analyses are heavily coloured by the dominant theme — the legitimization of the Welsh cultural distinctiveness — of the nationalist discourse, in which they played an important part.

The British community studies of the 1950s and early 1960s in general suffered from an unreflected acceptance of the *Gemeinschaft/Gesellschaft* dichotomy derived from the works of Durkheim, Tönnies, etc. This led to a projection of the ideal-types, community and society, on the realities of social life. Furthermore, the paradigms of the structural-functional approach, which dominated British social anthropology until the mid-1960s, also contributed to a misconstruction of community by anthropologists. Their preoccupation with structure — grounded in the structural-functionalist paradigm that structure determines behaviour — led to the misconception that structural change would inevitably lead to a loss of community or distinctiveness. However, the radical reassertion of the "community" by its members since the late 1960s has shown that structural discontinuity cannot be equated with loss of community or distinctiveness.

In this book I will discuss the development — the continuities and differences — within the social "science" discourse of community from the early structural-functionalist approaches of the 1940s and 1950s, to the introduction of symbolic anthropology into the field of community studies during "community studies revival" of the 1970s and 1980s. My intention is not to give a complete overview of the development of "anthropology at home" in Britain, rather, the first part of the book provides a general background to the discussion of community studies in Wales.

The cultural anthropologists, Arensberg and Kimball have been included because they have produced the first study of a community in the British Isles (Ireland) and their theoretical publications have influenced the approaches of social anthropologist working in Britain. For similar reasons Robert Redfield could not have been omitted. His concept of the rural-urban continuum developed in the mid-1950s returned in a slightly different form in Frankenberg's attempt to fit British communities into a morphological evolutionary and functional framework. Much room will be given to Frankenberg's study because it represented the first attempt to construct a theoretical framework for community studies in Britain, which had previously lacked explicit theoretical considerations.

During the mid-1970s social anthropology took up the challenge posed by a widespread tendency to cultural localism, which was a fight against the misrepresentation of the distinctive cultures of local communities in Britain by the centre. It was a paradigm change in anthropology which made it possible to see local communities not only in terms of structural features, which were certainly changing, but more as an interactive construct based on the people's experiences and their perceptions of their community. This led to the development of the theoretical concept of the symbolic construction of community by Anthony P. Cohen; a concept similar to Frederik Barth's theory of the construction and maintenance of ethnic identity which emphasized the crucial importance of boundaries in this process. Cohen argued that communities were able to maintain their distinctiveness in spite of the threat to their integrity, in the form of alien structural forms, because they were able to give these forms a new meaning which was more consonant with their own culture. Furthermore, distinctive structures of the community, which became obsolete as a result of the changes imposed from outside, were also infused with new meaning. Thus, the distinctiveness of the community was evident in meaning given to it by its members, rather than in its structure. He argued that the members of a community could maintain a certain sense of unity by the use of symbols, which are flexible enough to allow different interpretation by different individuals. The community finds its expression in the symbolic construction of its boundary; it is symbolically constituted through the process of deploying, interpreting and transforming symbols. This process is crucial for the maintenance of the community's distinctiveness because the knowledge of its symbolic repertoire cannot be controlled from outside.

The symbolic approach to the study of community, developed by Cohen, has been the most important development in the social anthropology of Britain in recent years. However, some of its problems will become evident in the discussion of the reflexivity debate concerning the anthropology "at home" which developed in the mid-1980s.

The second part of the book (chapter 7-9) is entirely devoted to the studies of Welsh culture. Wales has been chosen to represent the so-called *Celtic Fringe* because, firstly, the research of Welsh social geographers from the University College of Wales at Aberystwyth in mid-Wales on Welsh rural communities has contributed much to anthropological community studies in Britain; secondly, because I am familiar with an area of North Wales; thirdly, because the complex problems of the interrelationships between Welsh community and ethnic identity demonstrate clearly that the symbolic approach could contribute much to the understanding of the Welsh cultures. Furthermore, the early community studies of Welsh anthropologist can illustrate the problems of ideologically motivated distortion through idealization of community, which is inherent in the approaches of Tönnies and Durkheim; and the problems inherent in the structural-functionalist analysis of community.

2 THEORIES OF COMMUNITY

COMMUNITIES AS WHOLES, MICROCOSMS AND TYPES

Defining the object of study, the "tribe" or the "community", as an entity or a whole is an integral part of the "traditional" approach in social anthropology. It is, in a sense, a prerequisite for functionalist analysis of cultures as developed by Malinowski and Radcliffe-Brown. The main objective of functionalist analysis is to show the functional interdependencies of the parts or institutions of a society and their contribution to the maintenance of the society as a whole[2]. A social system, says Radcliffe-Brown (1952:181), has a functional unity in which all parts work together with a sufficient degree of harmony without producing unresolvable conflicts; it is, in short, a system in a state of equilibrium. "What people do, and say, and say they think, has a logical coherence and consistency that relates to the overall social structure of the community. Community life cannot continue successfully unless there is some such orderly structure of mutually reinforcing expectations and 'roles', some organization of interlocking parts which click together to form a harmonious whole." (Lewis 1985:20) It is quite obvious that Radcliffe-Brown was influenced by Durkheim's organism-analogy (see Lewis 1985:55)[3]. "Primitive societies were conceived of as closed systems, hard-surfaced, separate entities like billard balls. Very little attention was paid to the external interactions between these supposedly separate objects but, internally, each society was assumed to be integrated cohesively after the fashion of an organism or even a piece of clockwork." (Leach 1977:8) With regard to the structural-functional approach to community studies Margaret Stacey (1974:17) said that, "... there is no

---

2   What is meant here by society is human association in general and not *Gesellschaft*.
3   Bloch comments on Durkheim's influence on social anthropology: "It was only a very diluted and transformed version of Durkheim's work which influenced British anthropology, and this transformation was largely due to the other co-founder of the tradition with Malinowski, A. E. Radcliffe-Brown." (Bloch 1985:143)

good reason to suppose that everything is connected with everything else" and there is "...even less reason to suppose that this should be the case in any particular small locality of a nation state." To analyze a community, which is part of a complex industrial society, by simply declaring it to be an organic whole and not paying attention to its external relations does not only result in a misinterpretation of the community as such but it does also obscure our understanding of the social relationships within the community and its interconnectedness with the wider context[4]. The assumed wholeness or completeness of the so-called traditional rural community is an illusion, influenced by the ideological and emotional background of the anthropologist. The growing concern for the loss of distinctiveness of the local communities has quite clearly shown that the community is heavily influenced by forces external to it; centralization of power, higher mobility, nationwide mass media all have an influence on community life. Simpson (1974:314) said, that not only the social relationships of the members of a community extend beyond its boundaries, but also that "... the forces which integrate modern communities are likely to lie in organizations, both private and governmental, centred outside the community ..." If a community is so dependent on external factors "... it may be questionable whether a modern community *is* a unified whole in any real sense except that of geography."

The study of communities as microcosms is also based on the functionalist paradigm of the community as a well integrated whole. However, the American anthropologists Arensberg and Kimball (1974:337-338) argued that the functionalism of community studies was different from the "traditional" anthropological functionalism of Malinowski and Radcliffe-Brown which lead to an evaluation of customs and institutions in terms of their functional or dysfunctional quality. They abandoned such value categorization because they violated the inductive principles of what they called the "natural-history method". In the context of community studies, function is to be regarded as interdependence in the context of the whole. The study of community is based on the variability of relationships and not

---

4   A good example for this is A. D. Rees' (1950) study of Llanfihangel-yng-Ngwynfa. Although Rees mentioned the dependance on the English economy, he treated the community as if it was an isolated, well integrated whole. External (English) influences, for example, the spread of class solidarity based on common economic interest, were said to remain "... unintegrated with the wider complex of traditional culture." (Rees 1950:161; see pages 89-97)

upon the utility of an item of behaviour, structure or value to any other item. Community is seen as a kind of miniature society from which insights into macro-level social processes can be gained; "...community reveals the culture and society in which it occurs." (Arensberg & Kimball 1972:xi) Its study is the "...holistic examination of communities at the level of the social microcosm." (Ibid.:42) Arensberg and Kimball regarded the community as the "master social system" or "master institution" encompassing subsidiary systems. The "master social system" articulates five major subsidiary systems of community. These are the relationships of: (1) the familistic order; (2) age grading or generation, (3) sex organization, (4) local division of labour, (5) economic exchange and distribution (Arensberg & Kimball 1968:302-303). "These, then, comprise 'the framework of the social life in the countryside'. No event, they [Arensberg and Kimball] argue, can be understood without reference to them. The weakness of such grandiose claims has already been pointed out, but this form of structural-functional analysis was to be extremely influential on later studies, which were to continue this view of the countryside as essentially unchanging. This lead to some serious misinterpretations..." (Bell & Newby 1971:137). It was the community, or the "master social system", from which major insights into the connections between culture, society, and personality can be gained. Of all institutions of a society "... none is so central to continuity or determining of the larger structure and system as is the nexus of habitats, skills, norms, and interfunctioning roles we call here the community." (Arensberg & Kimball 1972:x) Community was assumed to provide "... a cell-like duplication; a repeated, stable form for the culture ..." (Ibid.:x) in time and space. Arensberg and Kimball's approach is based on three assumptions (Ibid.:3-4). The first is that community is a "master system", the second, that the community utilizes physical space in a characteristic fashion (settlement pattern) — they see a "general tendency for mutual congruency between social form and settlement pattern" — , and the third, that communities do not exist in a vacuum but are interrelated and engaged in cooperative activities with other communities, — "these linkages between communities make up the network called 'society' ". Central to the analysis of communities is the examination of environment, social form, and patterned behaviour as three functionally interdependent variables. From this follows that "... community should be viewed as systems comprising interaction regularities and cultural behavior in an environment context."

Arensberg and Kimball (Ibid.:15) assumed that the community is a stable and enduring entity, which can be distinguished from other human associations based on territoriality and land use exactly because of its repetitive character, wholeness, and inclusiveness. Furthermore, they saw it as the natural sample because it is the "... natural unit of the drama of successive repetitions of the life of an enduring culture and society." (Ibid.:18) The emphasis on the repetitive character makes it clear that processes through time are central to Arensberg and Kimball's theory of community. An appropriate definition of community must structure all relevant factors — spatial, ecological, demographic, and human geographical — in "some sort of wholeness", the "prime key" to which is the temporal dimension. The community "... is the structural social field of interindividual relationships unfolding through time." (Ibid.:17) Based on these assumptions they concluded that communities seem to be the basic units of social organization and cultural transmission within a society (Ibid.:20). Equivalent to the gene-pool, the community must be seen as the natural unit of cultural transmission because it contains the minimal population (two sexes and at least three generations) needed to carry and transmit the culture, and to re-enact the historically rooted cultural and institutional inventory. It, thereby, insures the continuity of the species and provides the functional reason for the universal existence of the community.

In order to achieve a more general understanding of human society they developed the community study method which is basically empirical and inductive. It "... is the exploration of human cultural, social, and group behavior *in vivo*, in natural setting, rather like natural history methods in biology and zoölogy." (Ibid.:42) Ideally it should have been just a "tool of social science, but not a subject matter" (Ibid.:30) using the community as a sample while not making it the object of study. Holistic understanding is the core of the community study method. The community is chosen as a field of study because it is a manageable unit for the use of participant observation. It must be a whole, which essentially means that the observation of a "full round of local life" and a representative sample of society and its members must be possible (Ibid.:30). The anthropologist must conceive all factors in their entity and examine all the interfunctioning local institutions without distinction of kind. The fact that they are convinced that the anthropologist does not prejudice the discovery of relevant factors relating to the problem (Ibid.:31), although, problems are taken to the field for referral to empirical reality and hypothesis are built from the empirical perception of interconnections of relevant phenomena (Ibid.:11), is due to their illusionary positivistic conception of the non-existence of a relationship between knowledge and interest. They said, that community studies must be grounded in sound prior theory of the community as an object, "for it presupposes that one knows and can isolate a community when one sees one ..." (Ibid.:31). But their basic, to a great extent biologistic, assumptions about what a community *is* — and its characteristics — are simply taken for granted, and not in the least critically questioned. How, then, can the community study method provide for the development of a better theory of the nature of the community as an object (see Ibid.:13). What Arensberg and Kimball have constructed is a kind of self-fulfilling prophecy. The sample is chosen on the basis of their basic assumptions. The empirical data gathered from it, so they say, can only be judged on the basis of "... completeness and consistency in making what is now coming to be called a 'model' of that field." (Ibid.:32) Based on the unwarranted assumption that a community is a whole, the model must be constructed accordingly. It is then compared with other "similar wholes" on the basis of a detailed examination of the functional relationships. Only then is the problem fitted into its "proper niche" within the model (see Ibid.:31). The problem is that the empirical data were gathered with the problem in mind; the appropriate "niche", therefore, was not found through the examination of the empirical data but was *a priori* defined through the selection of the sample[5]. It is difficult to imagine how this procedure can advance the search for a better theory of community. A theory that is basically evolutionary in perspective and whose main concern is the discovery of universal laws which govern the evolution of both animal and human communities is a regressive development and not an improvement on theory. Moreover, Arensberg and Kimball's attempt to insure comparability ended in a rather absurd revival of the culture-area concept (see Arensberg & Kimball 1972:75-93).

Another, similarly fruitless attempt, to place different communities in an analytical framework is the use of communities as types. The typological approach was also inspired by the "classical" theories of Durkheim and Tönnies (see, e.g., Redfield 1947:295). "The effort in this kind of research

---

5   Bell and Newby (1971:132) also remarked that Arensberg and Kimball choose a locality that was unlikely to disconfirm their hypothesis.

is to explain the wide range of behaviour on the basis of a simple classification scheme. Once a concept like Gemeinschaft, or folk, is invoked, everything falls into place." (Simpson 1974:316) But it is not only a way of classifying communities, it is also a theory of social change. Robert Redfield used his community studies to test the "general thesis that the progressive loss of isolation, when associated with an increase in heterogeneity, produces social disorganization, secularization and individualization." (Bell & Newby 1971:42) In order to classify the different communities the concept of the *folk-urban continuum* was developed by Redfield after his study of the community of Tepoztlán in Yucatan. The type of "primitive society" — or "folk society" as he preferred to call it (Redfield 1947:293, footnote 1) — was placed on one end of the continuum, the type of urban society on the other. These types were ideal-types, imaginary entities constructed for heuristic purposes (Redfield 1947:294). To conceptualize the community Redfield, once again, invoked the functionalist paradigm of the community as a well integrated whole. But he confused the imaginary whole constructed for heuristic purposes with the perception of the members of the community. He justified his concept of the community as a whole by saying that to the member of an isolated community it "... is a round of life, a small cosmos; the activities and the institutions lead from one into all the others so that to the native himself the community is not a list of tools and customs; it is an integrated whole." (Redfield 1955:10) It is not surprising that the classification of the communities was clearly biased because it was based on the characteristics of what he saw as the well integrated whole of *folk society* or *the little community*. Urban society, the other end of the continuum, was little more than a simple antithesis of folk society — "To identify the city with the opposite of the folk society is convenient by a simple negativing of the propositions that identify the folk society ..." (Redfield 1955:145). Very similar to Tönnies' concept of *Gemeinschaft*, the folk society is characterized as small, isolate, non-literate, homogeneous, and as having a strong sense of group solidarity (Redfield 1947:297). We are told that "...where the community begins and where it ends is apparent"; its distinctiveness is apparent to the outside observer because it is expressed through the group-consciousness of the members (Redfield 1955:4). The little community is homogeneous or "slow changing" because the "activities and states of mind" are alike for all its members regardless of age and sex differences and are repeated by each new generation (Redfield 1955:4). The behaviour is traditional, spontaneous, uncritical, and personal (Redfield 1947:299-300). Self-sufficiency is also a "defining quality" of the community; Redfield called it a "cradle-to-the-grave arrangement" which provides for all or most of the needs of its members. Like Durkheim, he assumed that the division of labour is confined to a division of sex (Redfield 1947:297). Status is ascriptive rather than achieved and kinship relations and institutions are the relevant categories of experience (Redfield 1947:300-301). Redfield's four basic "qualities — distinctiveness, smallness, homogeneity, and all providing self sufficiency — " thus define the ideal-type of community called the little community. But the qualities of the ideal-type are present in reality in different degrees — no "real" community can exactly match the ideal-type. What Redfield did to construct his folk-urban continuum, was to arrange the communities in a descending order according to the degree to which the qualities were not present. At the urban-end of the continuum very little of the qualities survived, instead new characteristics appeared, "impersonal institutions", "atomization", and "a new character structure" (Redfield 1955:5). Communities at an intermediate point on the scale, "peasant" or "partly urbanized rural communities", show signs of an intermingling of the two distinct styles, the folk way of life and the urban way of life. Both are assumed to be wholes which may be conceived as interpenetrating one another. The interpenetration is observable on the boundaries of the two, especially when the member of the community sees himself in relation and contrast to the world outside his own community (Redfield 1955:130). "So, in thinking about peasant communities or about partly urbanized rural communities, we begin to shape a form of thought that will conceive primitive folk, or peasant life as a general and abstract kind of living, as an imagined total structure, qualitatively different from the kind of living that comes to characterize towns and cities. We could perhaps see in the village two kinds of abstractly distinguishable kinds of life and kinds of communities, and see these, right in the village in relationship to each other." (Redfield 1955:131) To study the effects of change he would, therefore, construct a model of the "traditional social structure of the old days" and compare it with the transformations brought about by outside agencies representing the way of life of the towns and cities. The initialization of the process of change is conceived of as being external to the community. Thus, change enters the community stage as the "much larger social system" of the nation state "penetrating into the local structure" of the community (Redfield 1955:44).

The folk-urban continuum, "... though put to death by several writers on the subject ..." (Bell & Newby 1971:42) continued to exert its influence because it had "... the heuristic appeal of being a relatively simple way of conceptualizing social change and classifying communities." (Ibid.:46) A concept very similar to Redfield's *folk-urban continuum* was the *rural-urban continuum* developed and applied to British communities by Ronald Frankenberg. He was a member of the Manchester school (Kuper 1987:129) and the influence of the work of his colleagues, on the problem of urbanization in Africa, is evident. Max Gluckman's theory of social change and conflict, J. C. Mitchell's and J. A. Barnes' applications of network analysis are "key concepts" in the construction of the rural-urban continuum. His book on "Communities in Britain", first published in 1966, is quite clearly a work in the tradition of the Manchester school. It was the first serious attempt to place the findings of British community studies in a sociological framework (Owen 1986:102). This framework was the model of the *rural-urban continuum* against which he wanted to "measure the adequacy of our knowledge of real social life in different parts of Britain." (Frankenberg 1969:12). Like most of his colleagues he focused on the rural community[6] and gave three reasons for doing so: (1) the longing to get back to the country life is part of the national stereotype of ourselves; (2) nearly all of the community studies made since 1945 have concentrated on small (fewer than 50,000 inhabitants) communities; (3) community studies "can be a most fruitful source of knowledge about our own society." (Ibid.:11) Furthermore, he wanted to use his knowledge of the differences of, what he called, "truly rural" and "less rural" areas in the UK to achieve a better understanding of "what Britain is like", "what society in general is like" and of "the processes of social change" (Ibid.:12).

Social change was to be measured by the application of the model of the *rural-urban continuum*. The continuum served as a scale on which the different communities could be arranged; but it was only morphological "... because although each state is structurally more complicated than the one before, and each has a more diversified economy and technology, there is no necessary implication that..." a rural village will become successively like a less rural town. Frankenberg has tried to combine the

---

6 "This is a book about Britain and British communities. Four fifths of the population of Britain live in towns with a population of over fifty thousand. A half of these live in the six great conurbations. This book is mainly about the social behaviour of the other fifth. Why is this minority worth focusing on?" (Frankenberg 1969:11)

morphological evolutionary and the functional approach. To overcome the difficulty of the functional approach to carry procedures to their logical conclusion and to assemble the data systematically when dealing with people, one must first of all know to what items of behaviour functions are being imputed. Furthermore, it is equally important to distinguish between what an actor expects to happen as a result of his actions (subjective dispositions) and what actually happens (objective consequences). But no society is totally homogeneous; all communities studied are divided by class and status. It follows that, behaviour which is functional in one situation, or for one group, may not be functional in another situation, or for another group. "Nor is the external or internal structure necessarily stable; it is subject like everything else to change. What is functional today may have a different function tomorrow or be even dysfunctional."

He did not think of the continuum as a straight evolutionary line, but rather a "messy squiggle, blurred here and sharp there. ... Nevertheless, I think the tendency of direction of change is clear." His idea of the direction of change and the application of the *rural-urban continuum* was based on six "key concepts": community, role, network, class and status-group, conflict, and social redundancy (Ibid.:237). Through the incorporation of role, network, conflict, and social redundancy the concept of the rural- or folk-urban continuum was certainly refined.

The concept of community is defined by several interconnected factors. A community must be small enough so that its members can meet frequently and engage in face-to-face interaction. Members of a community have "overriding economic interests which are the same or complementary." (Ibid.:238)

Although the community's economy may be simple, its social life is very complex. For people living in a small rural community it is seldom possible to play one role at a time because the community suffers from "a shortage of actors to perform all available roles" (Ibid.:239), which means that the individual must master the difficult task to enact different roles simultaneously. Playing a role can be understood as acting according to a part, a social position, assigned to each individual by society. A role implies an audience or a number of different audiences. Each requires the playing of a different role, consequently the total role is made up of many, often contradictory, roles — "A schoolteacher as a schoolteacher relates to pupils, to the governors of the school, the headmaster, the school-caretaker, and several others." Each social position has not one role expected of him/her but many; each group or individual he/she interacts with has different expectations of him/her which will lead to unavoidable conflict. The individual will try to resolve this conflict by trying to meet the expectations of the most important other member in his/her role-set. In rural society "... the performers of other roles in an individual's many role-sets are likely to be the same people." (Ibid.:240) There is less opportunity to hide ones performance from the other members of the role-set because the role-sets overlap and all roles tend to be played in public. Thus, the conflicting expectations are more likely to become apparent and disputes are more likely to break out. But there are special mechanisms which minimize the outbreak of conflicts and may even turn conflicts into a cohesive force. Frankenberg contrasted the role relationships of the rural community with those of the city. In the city each individual also plays many roles but to different audiences. City-dwellers have less interests in common because the economy is diversified and complicated (Ibid.:241). He called it "the complexity of community life as against the complication of the city. I see complexity changing to complication as technological diversity causes and results from the division of labour." (Ibid.:242) At this point, I believe, the concept of social redundancy comes in. Redundancy is a concept borrowed from communication theory. "Cherry defines it as 'a property of languages, codes and sign systems which arises from a superfluidity of rules, and which facilitates communication in spite of all the factors of uncertainty acting against it.' " (Ibid.:280) The desire to be correctly understood promotes redundancy because it reduces the risk of misunderstandings through the communication of more than the actually necessary amount of information. Rural communities, says Frankenberg, show greater redundancy; the role relationships are "redundantly contaminated by the content of other role relationships" (Ibid.:280). A small number of role relationships is arranged with greater fluidity into varied patterns. In urban societies redundancy does not disappear but it changes. Urban social life makes up for the loss of fluidity with a large number of role relationships and their formalization. (Ibid.:282-283)

Referring to Erving Goffman he distinguished between role-commitment and role-attachment. The commitment to certain roles, he said, lies "in the nature of society"; people are committed to them whether they like it or not. Role-attachment, on the other hand, involves a certain degree of choice. In rural communities the individual is more likely to become attached to the roles he/she is committed to by birth (ascribed roles); to describe such a member of a community he uses the term local. Cosmopolitan members of a community are also committed to roles but are not attached to them and thus try to reduce their commitment. "In urban societies, individuals still have ascribed roles but add to them achieved roles. They are committed to both but are more likely to be attached to the latter." (Ibid.:242) Later in his discussion of roles he referred to the division in the industrial working class of both Banbury and Glossop (less rural communities) in terms of locals and cosmopolitans. The locals are committed as well as attached to their subordinate role, the cosmopolitans are merely committed and will try to change the content of the role. "I would expect that workers would tend to *embrace* their role in rural society and to *reject* it in urban. In other words, *all* the working class who remain in rural areas are locally oriented." (Ibid.:263)

Another important concept for his rural-urban continuum is the network. He followed J. A. Barnes (1969) in distinguishing three social fields: locality, occupation, and personal network. The personal network is ego centred, made up of personal ties (friends) and overlaps with other personal networks. In rural communities the network tends to be close-knit, which means that most of the networks overlap — everybody is in some way connected to everybody else. The chances that the networks overlap in urban society is small and, thus, the personal network tends to be loose-knit (Ibid.:243-244). He also made use of Elizabeth Bott's application of the network-model to the problem of role relationships in urban families. Frankenberg placed Bott's three types of family organization[7] in a continuum ranging from highly segregated (complementary) to joint role relationships. To illustrate his concept he referred to the process of child rearing which sharpens the division of labour between husband and wife. At the community-end of the scale the wife's dependence on her own kin increases, while the husband, "his wife's attention absorbed elsewhere, may be drawn back to the peer group companions he forsook at courtship and marriage." (Ibid.:246) At the other end of the scale the couple is more isolated and may be forced into a more joint role relationship by the dependence on each other. "Secondly, the change in the pattern of men's

---

7 (1) *complementary family organization* — activities of wife and husband are different and separate but form a whole; (2) *independent family organization* — activities of wife and husband have no reference to each other; (3) *joint family organization* — activities are carried out by wife and husband together. (Frankenberg 1969:244-245).

lives from rural-agricultural to industrial-urban is much greater than that in women's." (Ibid.:246)

Frankenberg concluded that the factors which influence the connectedness of social networks in towns are "the mechanisms that are associated with the tendency towards the progressive loosening of networks as we proceed from country to town." (Ibid.:247) Firstly, kinship ties are strengthened by common economic interest; secondly, the neighbourhood is characterized by a dominant local industry or a small number of traditional local occupations; thirdly, the lack of physical and social mobility gives little opportunity to make relationships outside the existing network.

Frankenberg's idea of the rural-urban continuum was influenced by Aidan Southall's (1959) concept of the rural-urban continuum developed for the analysis of African towns — he believed that Southall's idea of the continuum united the concept of the role and the network[8]. Southall (1973:72) argued that cities, because of their enormous range in size, function and culture, cannot be fitted onto any absolute measure but only on a continuum. "To envisage a continuum from rural to urban social structure is to envisage a special case of the continuum from simple to complex society. It is necessary to consider, as far as possible, the whole range of rural social structures and the whole range of urban social structures, not just the extreme instances of either. The basis of the continuum is the density of role-relationships, the significance of which is amplified by the changes in the balance of qualitative aspects and types of role-relationships which accompany increasing density. It is assumed that increasing density of role-relationships accompanies any transition, temporal or spatial, from rural to urban social structure." (Southall 1973:83) The rural-end of the Southall's continuum is characterized by a *low density role texture*, which means a low population density, broad roles, diffuse role definition, overt role development, equality of role distribution, and long standing role relationships. The urban-end is characterized by a *high density role texture*, which means a high population density, narrow roles, specific role definition, latent role development, inequality of role distribution, and ephemeral role relationships (Frankenberg 1969:251). Broad roles are defined as cutting across all five major type categories of roles. "These are: (i) kinship and ethnic, (ii) economic, (iii) political, (iv) ritual and

---

[8] Frankenberg was, indeed, applauded by Southall (1973:84) for the successful application of his criteria.

religious, and (v) recreational. ... In rural society (and still more in tribal society) any role is likely to splay across all five of these areas of activity." (Ibid.:249) But the boundaries of the five categories tend to be blurred in a rural community. In urban society where they are more clearly defined, the roles are narrow, limited to one or a few of the five categories at a time; however, they are never, in any society, watertight (Ibid.:249). There is also a development from overt — mediated by direct face-to-face interaction in rural communities — to latent role relationships in urban society which never bring the participants face-to-face (e.g. prejudices, voting patterns, voluntary associations). Finally, there are the criteria of the degree of inequality of distribution and the duration of role relationships. Ideally, everyone in rural communities has an equal opportunity to interact with everyone else but even at the rural end of Frankenberg's continuum, rural Ireland and Wales, the division of labour has cut the women off from full interaction. In rural communities role relationships are characterized by the relative continuity of roles, in urban society the constant population change makes the roles more temporary (Ibid.:250-251).

In relation to class and status Frankenberg followed the classical concepts of Marx and Weber. Max Gluckman's concept of conflict was also utilized in the analysis of class. Maurice Bloch (1985:144) remarked that, although conflict in Gluckman's sense would not normally be seen as class conflict, his pupils, such as Frankenberg, reintroduced the idea of class under the label of conflict. Referring to Marx, Frankenberg said that the nature of class relations can be discovered through an examination of the differences in relationships to the means of production. He was "...particularly interested in Marx's views on class for it was he who saw that the struggle between the classes created social change, and he was particularly concerned with the increasing divergence of rural and urban societies." (Ibid.:255) Frankenberg also saw class as a dynamic concept which changes in different social situations. Classes are not always engaged in struggle and in "relatively stable periods of history class differences may become blurred by status, or routinized into institutions which assume a conservative function." (Ibid.:256) Referring to Weber he said that a status group is characterized by a "particular concept of status honour and the adoption of a particular style of life." (Ibid.:259) Class and status groups are stratified according to two different principles. The first, according to their relations to the production and acquisition of goods, the second, according to the principles of consumption based on a special style of life (Ibid.:261-262).

Status in rural society is total because it is the result of daily face-to-face interaction — status decides how one interacts, in urban society it is not because "... in the town considerations of status determine with whom interaction takes place — status decides whether." (Ibid.:263)

In accordance with Max Gluckman's concept of conflict as a cohesive force[9] Frankenberg assumed that "... the social mobility of individuals emphasizes the class system through which they move. Individual rebellion against class, especially if successful, may serve merely to reassert class values...". Thus the social mobility between classes serves to strengthen the class system as a whole (Ibid.:264). On the whole he suggested that in rural communities "...conflict is more omnipresent and more likely to be disruptive if it breaks into open dispute. At the same time, the nature of such societies enables, if it does not demand, the channeling and institutionalizing of conflict in such a way that the occasion of dispute becomes the occasion of coherence. The contrast can be expressed in the terms that in rural communities there are divisions but no fundamental cleavages; there are rebellions but not revolutions. The end-point of such rebellions is an immediate reassertion of the values and unity of the group." (Ibid.:270-271)

His theory of social change, the rural-urban continuum, is based on Marx's concept of the alienation of the worker in the labour process and the alienation from his product of labour[10]. Alienation by economic change, said Frankenberg, will then lead to an alienation from the cultural goals of society because these "... goals and aims of society are set in a way that makes them incapable of achievement by the majority of the population." (Ibid.:277) Society has reached a state of anomie[11] which will lead to an alienation from norms. He said that, both Durkheim and Marx "... saw the conflicts arising out of alienation and anomie as destructive conflicts which, far from maintaining social cohesion, were instruments of social change." (Ibid.:278) But this is a misinterpretation, or at least a simplification, of both Marx's and Durkheim's ideas. In Durkheim's view the anomic

---

9   See, for example, Gluckman 1963.
10 Giddens refers to the "two directly related but partially separable sources of alienation in the capitalist mode of production" as "technological alienation" and "market alienation". (Giddens 1971:228)
11 He uses Merton's and not Durkheim's definition of anomie. Merton states that it is "a dissociation between culturally prescribed aspirations and socially structured avenues for realizing these aspirations." (Merton in Frankenberg 1969:277)

RURAL	URBAN (less rural)
Community	Association
Social fields involving few	Social fields involving many
Multiple role relationships	Overlapping role relationships
Role conflict within a role set	Role conflict in different role sets
Simple economy	Diverse economy
Little division of labour	Extreme differentiation and specialization
Mechanical solidarity	Organic solidarity
Complexity	Complication
Ascribed status	Achieved status
Status	Contract
Total status	Partial status
Education form status	Status from education
Role embracement	Role commitment
Small mesh, or close-knit, networks	Large mesh, or loose-knit, networks
Locals	Cosmopolitans
Low density role texture	High density role texture
Economic class - one division among many	Economic class - dominating social life through the cash nexus
Latent function	Manifest function
Relations of conjunction and disjunction	Segregation of conflicting groups
Organization by general unanimity	Organization by voting system
Conflict and rebellion	Cleavage and revolution
Regional focus of life	Occupational focus of life
Integration	Alienation and estrangement
Acceptance of norms and conflict within consensus	Normlessness, alienation from norms, or anomie
Changing pattern of social redundancy	

Fig. 1 Frankenberg's rural-urban continuum.

state of modern industry which produced a moral vacuum does not necessarily result in destructive conflict or a radical reorganization of the social order. Durkheim emphasized the importance of cumulative changes for societal development, whereas Marx emphasized revolutionary dynamism (Giddens 1971:203-204) Like Marx, Durkheim also recognized the problem of the dehumanizing or alienating effect of the modern labour process. "But whereas Durkheim's proposals for the reduction or eradication of this dehumanisation of the worker are based upon the moral consolidation of specialisation in the division of labour, Marx's hope and expectation is that this division of labour will itself be radically changed. This is really the crux of the most significant differences between Marx's use of the conception of alienation and Durkheim's employment of the notion of anomie." (Giddens 1971:230) Though Frankenberg, like most community sociologists and anthropologists, "... has utilized assertions of the alienating effects of society, the dehumanizing character of mass society ... as the significant characteristic of modern western society ..." (Gusfield 1975:20), he did not see a solution for the problem of alienation in the return to the community. He said: "I am not arguing that village life is 'better' than that of the town. To do so would be to condemn all those people who flowed into the towns from the beginning of the nineteenth century onwards as irrational .... Nor, however, do I personally believe that the life of modern English towns or cities is perfect and cannot be improved. I do not think there is any possibility of returning to village life even if we wanted to. In my view the gains of urban life, actual and potential, are infinitively greater than the losses. I would rather [sic] enough cubic feet of housing space and an efficient milkman than three acres of land and a cow." (Frankenberg 1969:285)

3 VOYAGE INTO THE BLACK (W)HOLE

THE SOCIAL ANTHROPOLOGY OF BRITAIN IN THE 1950s AND 1960s

Little anthropological research on European societies was done before the 1950s. The few studies which were carried out during the late 1920s and 1930s — e.g. Conrad M. Arensberg's (1968) study of rural southern Ireland (County Clare), C. G. Chapman's (1971) study of rural Sicily, and I. Sanders' (1949) account of rural life in south-eastern Europe — were exclusively about rural societies on the margins of Europe. "Only those peoples who appeared to be most marginal to the mainstream of European civilization, and thus not fully European at all, were recognized as fit objects for anthropological comparison." (Cole 1977:352) Thus, an image of these "marginal" and "traditional" European communities was created which fitted the notion of "primitive societies" as close as possible. Like their predecessors (Marx, Durkheim, Tönnies, etc.) at the end of the last century modern anthropologists had particular ideas about their own modern societies, and community came to replace the tribe as the "primitive" opposite of modern society. "The desire to be as primitive as every other colleague ..." says Davis (1977:7), may be responsible for some of the failures of European community studies, including the problem of marginality and the ignorance of the links between rural and urban, the community and its wider context (e.g. the state). In addition to that, European anthropologists were not taken seriously by their colleagues because they did not experience a complete cultural disorientation which may sharpen the anthropologist's sense of the problematic and have taken certain forms of social organization, like the family, for granted. Most social anthropologists seemed to think "... that anthropology is only anthropology if it is done very much abroad, in unpleasant conditions, in societies which are very different from the ethnographer's native habitat, very different from the sort of place where he might go on holiday." (Davis 1977:7)

However, "primitive society" is no longer the object of study; social anthropology is no longer concerned with the *primitive* in contrast to the modern and not necessarily with *the other* far away from home (Kuper 1988:243). Mainstream social anthropology parted from the idea of the "primitive" some time ago but it certainly was still prominent in the thinking of the community anthropologists who undertook research in the 1950s and 1960s. Instead of being thousands of miles away *the other* was located more conveniently *around the corner* — in the UK the so-called "Celtic Fringe", for example, proved to be sufficiently removed from the mainstream of British society and "traditional" (which is a very thin disguise for "primitive") enough to be worth studying. In that sense, the concept "community" in British social anthropology had retained a lot of the characteristics of the concept of "primitive society". The survival of the idea of the "primitive society" may be due to the persistence of the structural-functionalist theories in British social anthropology. This is true for the anthropological community studies until the 1960s. In the next chapter we will see that the rationale for studying remote or peripheral areas changed considerably during the 1970s and 1980s.

Until the mid 1960s — a time when "structural-functionalism was in deep trouble" because everyone was looking for new approaches (Jackson 1987:8) — British social anthropology was dominated by the structural-functionalist paradigms which were essentially developed immediately before the war (see Kuper 1987:141). However, most of the anthropological community studies are devoid of any explicit theoretical considerations whatsoever. The functionalist postulate that a "traditional society" has to be conceptualized as a functional unity, a closed system, a whole — Leach's notorious "billard balls" (see page 11) — was mostly taken for granted without further reflection. The discussion of the meaning of community, its theoretical background and its methodological implications seems to have been regarded as a past-time for sociologists. Social anthropologists rarely entered the arena and, thus, left it to the sociologists to complain about the lack of theory in anthropological studies of community.

Generations of *sociologists* have tried to figure out what is meant by the "apparently elegant but infuriatingly slippery notion" (Hamilton 1985:7) of community. A definition of the concept seems to be impossible and by the 1970s an "exhaustion" (Bell & Newby 1971:32) concerning the search for an appropriate definition of the term had been reached. "Over the years it has proved to be highly resistant to satisfactory definition in anthropology and sociology, perhaps for the simple reason that all definitions contain or imply theories, and the theory of community has been very contentious." (Cohen 1985a:11) In 1971 Bell and Newby[12] simply gave up: "Rather as intelligence is what intelligence tests measure perhaps we can, for the time being at any rate, merely treat community as what community studies analyze." (Bell & Newby 1971:32) A few years later, in an article with Saunders and Rose (Bell et. al. 1978:55), they entirely dismissed the concept of community as ambiguous and theoretically misleading. Charsley (1986:173) has also warned us, that if the measures used to define the community are problematic, "... the anthropologist may well be suspicious of the ontological status of the entity which requires such measures for its identification. It has indeed long been apparent that the term carries such a burden of ambiguous connotation and sentiment that its value as an analytic term has to be doubtful." Community is a long established referent in the rhetoric of both politicians and "scientists" that derives its power "... largely from its very ambiguity which is its major drawback as a technical term." During the 1950s, when Hillery tried to find the common ground in 94 community definitions (Hillery 1955), the attitude towards the problem seemed to be rather more optimistic. Nevertheless, the areas of agreement elicited by Hillery were rather banal: 73 of the 94 community definitions included a combination of social interaction, area and some common ties as the necessary elements of community. For one of the 73 definitions only area and social interaction were relevant criteria, whilst three defined community only through social interaction and common ties (Bell & Newby 1971:29). It is quite obvious that the result of Hillery's labourious attempt was rather useless for cutting a path through the jungle of community definitions. In conclusion we can only say, that there was — and still is — little agreement about what a community *is* [13]. In fact, until Frankenberg's *Communities in Britain,* British social anthropologists seemed to have regarded the question of how to define a community not as a necessary question to be reflected upon. In social anthropology there was

---

12 Day and Murdoch (1993:83-84) believe that: "Bell and Newby's textbook account of this tradition (1971) turned out to be, in effect, its death knell. Rather than inspiring a new wave of case studies in community research, it seemed to provide ample justification for ignoring past work of the kind."
13 Cohen (1985a:38) comments on Hillery's rather unproductive attempt: "Community studies were con signed for some time into an abyss of theoretical sterility by obsessive attempts to formulate precise analytic definitions (see, for example Hillery, 1955)."

"an early efflorescence" (Jackson 1987:10) of research in Britain in the 1950s, especially under Little at Edinburgh and Rees at Aberystwyth. As late as 1966, Frankenberg (1966:11) expressed the opinion that community studies "... can be a most fruitful source of knowledge about our own society." But the late 1960s were also the time of a weakening confidence in the value of community studies.

The early studies of British rural communities have all shared the implicit acceptance of the community-society dichotomy. This typology, originally derived from the works of Durkheim, Tönnies, etc., is not only the most relevant (see page 7) but also the most dangerous theoretical concept used in the study of complex industrial societies. Its danger lies in the confusion of the ideal-types, community and society — constructed by the analyst to make sense of the empirical data and to communicate them — with the real world. Community and society are analytical terms and not empirical descriptions representing reality. Furthermore, the exclusiveness of both types is potentially misleading because no human association is purely communal or societal. Furthermore, Cohen (1985:24) claimed that the notion of exclusiveness, or historical incompatibility, of mechanical and organic solidarity was the result of a misinterpretation of Durkheim's thoughts. "In the current sociological usage, the concepts of 'community and society' have emerged as opposites in an almost zero-sum form. That is, whatever accentuates society diminishes community, and vice versa. The sum is zero. Reality is made out to be one *or* the other; communal *or* societal." (Gusfield 1975:13) The second serious problem of the typology is the fallacy of taking ideologically based constructs as reality. Community has often been, and still is, imbued with nostalgia for the *good old days* of close-knit, harmonious, emotionally supporting human relationships in contrast to the alienation which is supposed to be characteristic of present day society[14]. "Community studies carried out in Europe have constructed an object based on normative notions and bolstered by assumptions which are taken for granted." (Ennew 1980:1) Moreover, they also tended to ignore the political and economic realities of the state but, at the same time, implicitly criticized urban industrial society. Even Frankenberg, although he emphasized that gains of modern urban society, contributed to the mystification of the community. The "truly rural" society is charac-

---

14 A good example for community as a romanticized ideal and normative prescription is again Rees's study of *Life in a Welsh countryside* (Rees 1950; for a detailed account of Rees's study see pp. 89-97).

terized by integration whereas the "less rural" or urban society is characterized by alienation and estrangement. The estrangement of modern man from his fellow human beings is seen as the consequence of the development from "truly rural" (community) to "less rural" (society). "In this shape, the typology of community and society is not only an empirical usage, it is also a *mythical device* which expresses a present emotion." (Gusfield 1975:88, emphasis added) Symes (1981:27) argues that the community-society dichotomy was more appropriate to the conditions of the nineteenth century when the gap between rural and urban areas was great and interaction between these areas weak. The relations of town and country in the twentieth century, however, are different because increased mobility and population exchange have resulted in a convergence of urban and rural life styles. The "... modification of the Gemeinschaft - Gesellschaft dichotomy in favour of the rural-urban continuum linking the two ideal-types and implying that significant discontinuities no longer exist..." (Symes 1981:27, emphasis removed) has taken account of the different conditions of twentieth century society. But, I believe, the assumption that significant discontinuities no longer exist is an illusion which was generated in Frankenberg's case by his preoccupation with structure. The notion of discontinuity presupposes that structure determines behaviour — which, in fact, is a paradigm of structural-functionalism — and that similar structural influences produce similar behaviour (see Cohen 1985a:36). Furthermore it implies the presupposition that structure also determines identity. But the idea of continuity or dis-continuity, as expressed by Frankenberg, can only relate to a change in form or appearance and not to a change of meaning and identity. In the second chapter I will try to show that evolutionary scales, like the rural-urban continuum, and the resulting postulates of continuity or dis-continuity are misconceptions of the process of social change. Structural discontinuity cannot be equated with loss of community or distinctiveness as the radical reassertion of "the community" by its members has clearly shown.

Nevertheless, Frankenberg's book on "Communities in Britain" was loudly applauded as the first attempt to construct a framework within which the different communities in Britain could be placed — but the concept of rural-urban continuum was henceforth ignored! It is symptomatic that Anthony Jackson (1987:11), in his "Reflections on ethnography at home and the ASA", when explaining that anthropological community studies were discrete and idiosyncratic and of no use to grand sociological theory, only said that Frankenberg had given "a good account of such studies as were done in Britain", but never mentioned the rural-urban continuum. I believe that Frankenberg's rural-urban continuum can possibly be seen as the first and the last attempt of British social anthropology to fit community studies in Britain into a kind of sociological framework and thereby hope to proceed on the road to grand sociological theory.

There is yet another dichotomy which has to be mentioned: the social anthropology-sociology dichotomy. Sociologists seem to think that social anthropologists when studying their own society have trespassed on the field owned by sociology. So, it comes as no surprise, that those social anthropologists who studied their own society and tried hard to become as scientific as their sociologist colleagues referred to themselves as sociologists. "One obvious reason why the term 'anthropologist' is so unwelcome is that it is associated with colonialism (and the preservation of tribalism — the anathema of all modern states), while the label 'sociologist' denotes a scientific examination of one's own society for its own good, since sociology is closely linked to notions of social welfare and progress — misplaced as this notion may be." (Jackson 1987:7)

The conflict, or the misunderstanding, between sociology and social anthropology is a fundamental one and philosophical in nature. While social anthropologists have abandoned the idea of a universal theory about the evolution of human societies and emphasize the hermeneutic nature of anthropology, the sociologist feared to do so "... since it would undermine the whole rationale for their existence." (Ibid.) Many sociologists seem to suffer from a violent allergic reaction when social anthropological research at home is mentioned — very much like Count Dracula when confronted with garlic. It is held to be "... too idiosyncratic and subjective in character and, therefore, nearer the art-form of the novel than the scientific treatise." (Owen 1986:41) Idiosyncracy and subjectivity are attributed to the use of "uncritical anthropological techniques" (Bell & Newby 1971:63). These techniques, so they say, were designed for the study of non-literate peoples and are not adequate for studying advanced industrial societies. The collection of empirical data by participant observation and the subsequent involvement of the anthropologist in community life is criticized as "overinvolved", "partial", and not "detached". "This sharing of experience is not, of course, always conducive to the supposed ideal detachment of the scientist." (Bell & Newby 1971:55) Bell and Newby have some rather strange ideas about the study of the so-called "non-literate people" and the role of the anthropologist. They assume that there may be a place for the anthropologist in the social structure of "some North American Indian groups" — these groups "... are now *said to have* put their anthropologist on their genealogies ..." —, whereas "... most communities have no place in their social structure for the sociologist." (Bell & Newby 1971:55, emphasis added) What they seem to be saying is that it is easier to become a member of a "primitive tribe", despite the cultural and ethnic differences, than it is to become a member of a community. By doing this they become subject to their own criticism; like communities in "advanced industrial societies" these "North American Indian groups" *do not* exist in a vacuum — they are also part of the so-called "advanced industrial society". It is very interesting, and symptomatic of the ignorance of most sociologists, that Bell and Newby obtained their ideas about anthropology from an article published by Robert Bierstadt on "The limitations of anthropological methods in sociology" in the American Journal of Sociology which dates from 1948-1949![15] When Owen (1986:41) criticized the anthropological studies of Welsh communities as being "...nearer the art-form of the novel than the scientific treatise" he was, in a way, correct but missed the point; the ethnographic "novel" — if it can convey the insights, the deep understanding, of the anthropologist — might contribute more to the understanding of oneself and other people than the scientific treatise. I very much agree with Edmund Leach's view that social anthropology "... is not, and should not aim to be, a 'science' in the natural science sense. If anything it is a form of art." (Leach 1986:52) Therefore, the social anthropologist can only be a kind of novelist and never become a scientist. Sociologists, and even some anthropologists, who strive hard to become "real scientists" should bear Anthony Jackson's statement in mind: "If Leach's view of the subjective nature of ethnographies is correct it applies to all anthropologists (both at home and abroad) and, by the same token, to sociologists as well. This could explain why sociology has now fallen from official favour since it could never deliver what it promised about understanding social problems." (Jackson 1987:11)

If anthropology is a form of art we must ask how it can achieve a deeper understanding (not an *explanation*) of the processes of change — for the

---

15 Only one year later Evans-Pritchard wrote that anthropologists could no longer ignore history because the communities which they study are enclosed in and part of "great historical societies" (Evans-Pritchard 1962:21).

study of communities in the modern world is necessarily a study of change. In the next chapter we will examine the results of the "...introspective look at what social anthropologists, themselves, are doing as a discipline in terms of theory and methodology..." (Jackson 1987:9) in regard to the study of their own society.

4 THE REVIVAL OF COMMUNITY STUDIES

When, in the 1970s, social anthropologists rediscovered the study of rural communities in Britain as a worthwhile subject, the results were far from revolutionary. Nevertheless, the new studies "... awakened new interest in the 'taken-for-granted' acceptance of things in small communities and their perceived problems." (Jackson 1987:11) In 1981 and 1982 the first major anthropological contributions to community studies since the late 1960s were published. The first book was Marilyn Strathern's (1981) account of the Essex village of Elmdon, *Kinship at the Core*, and the second book was *Belonging* (Cohen 1982a), the first volume of a new series of *Anthropological Studies of Britain*. McFarlane has shown that these two publications encouraged other anthropologists to do fieldwork in local communities: "Cohen's (1982) and Strathern's (1981) gestures of defiance towards those who criticise the analytical (if not descriptive) power of community study were, and are, heartening for those of us who are aware of the cultural salience of the locality in people's lives." (McFarlane 1986:88) However, the interest of social anthropologists in doing fieldwork "at home" was still small during the 1970s. When the first volume of the *Anthropological Studies of Britain* was planned in 1978 the most difficult problem was the scarcity of recent anthropological research on communities in the British Isles. Even though the number of social anthropologists doing fieldwork in Europe was increasing, the number of anthropologists doing fieldwork at home was still small — an analysis of the theoretical and regional interest of ASA (Association of Social Anthropologists of the Commonwealth) members, living or working in Britain in 1981, showed that only 36 out of 171 stated Britain as their field of regional interest (Kuper 1987:206-207).

In the preface to the second volume of the *Anthropological Studies of Britain* Cohen has described the slow process of reorientation:

"After the demise of the brilliant urban and rural community studies of the 1950s and 1960s, anthropologists paid little attention to studies of indigenous British cultures. Even while the focus of social anthropology was widening to embrace the industrialised societies, work on Britain tended to limp along as an obscure, minority activity. During the early 1970s, a mere handful of British scholars were thus engaged. But, later in the decade, interest burgeoned, particularly among postgraduate students. Since then, more seasoned professionals have also redirected their scholarly attention to work within Britain." (Cohen 1986a:viii)

The scholarly attention was quite clearly focused on the peripheral areas of the British Isles and particularly the so-called Celtic Fringe. In his assessment of the decline of community studies in sociology, Bulmer (1985:431) stated "... that anthropological studies of the Celtic fringe remain an exception to the overall generalisation about the decline of this type of study ...". In 1982 *Belonging* was published, and except for Marilyn Strathern's (1982a, 1982b) study of Elmdon (Essex) all the studies presented were studies of rural communities in the so-called Celtic Fringe [16]. The studies compiled in the second volume, *Symbolising Boundaries*, published in 1986 (Cohen 1986a), were also mostly concerned with peripheral communities. Cohen (1987:213) argued that the preoccupation of anthropologists with the peripheral areas of the British Isles in the 1970s was justified because these areas were "ideal vantage points" for the observation of social change. "Their distance from the political and economic 'centres' was clearly a matter of culture rather than merely of geography, a distance which both contributed to and was exacerbated by ignorance or misunderstanding about them by those in the 'centre'. But one was castigated for seeking to replicate anthropological 'bush' in an industrialised economy, for confusing cultural boundaries (bourgeois mystification) with those of class; for bucolic romanticism; for downright irrelevance."

A quite unusual project by orthodox standards of anthropological fieldwork was the study of the Essex village of Elmdon from 1962 until 1977 (see Strathern 1981, 1982a, 1982b and Robin 1980). The village, only 14 miles from Cambridge, was studied by students from the Department of Social Anthropology, University of Cambridge under the supervision of Edmund Leach and Audrey Richards for short periods of time (rarely more than a week or two). The project was unusual for anthropologists because

---

16 Whalsay, Shetland and Clachan, Lewis in Scotland; Tory Island in the Republic of Ireland and Kilbroney in Northern Ireland; Blaenau Ffestiniog, Gwynedd in Wales.

of the long duration (15 years) and the discontinuity of the fieldwork which made real participant observation impossible. Only Audrey Richards, who had lived permanently in the village from 1964 onwards (temporarily since 1957), provided some continuity for the whole project (Richards 1981). The data collected during the 15 years of fieldwork by various students and Audrey Richards were analyzed by Marilyn Strathern, who had been an initial member of the project in 1962, and published in her remarkable account of Elmdon life and "English" culture, *Kinship at the Core*, in 1981.

Astonishingly, Wales, the focus of anthropological interest during the late 1940s and the 1950s, has been virtually left untouched by the community studies revival of the 1970s — one exception is Emmett's work on Blaenau Ffestiniog (see Emmett 1978, 1982a, 1982b). Scotland, on the other hand, has received more attention; it was a focus of research during the 1970s and 1980s[17].

Undertaking ethnographic research "at home" became increasingly popular with British anthropologists during the 1970s and 1980s. The factors which influenced the revival of the interest in studying indigenous communities in the British Isles were very diverse and complex. In his résumé of anthropological research in Britain, Anthony Jackson (1987:8-9) presented six practical reasons for the revival:

" 1. Decreased funding.
2. Increased student numbers.
3. Objections by many new states to research into what they call 'tribalism' and a suspicion of neo-colonial intellectual imperialism.
4. The discovery of large areas of ignorance about one's own society.
5. The current interest shown by historians in using anthropological insights to interpret past records.
6. The ease of access to one's own society and a reduction of the time and money needed to enter the field." [18]

Although significant, these reasons can provide only a partly explanation. Another, probably the most important, factor was the change in British

---

17 For Example: Cohen's research in the Shetland island community of Whalsay, Peter G. Mewett's (1982a, 1982b, 1983, 1986, 1988) and Judith Ennew's (1979, 1980) fieldwork in the Hebrides.
18 Cole (1977:356, footnote 3) has speculated that the British interest in Europe might have been tied to "...the switch from Britain's status as a world colonial power to a relatively underdeveloped member of the European common market."

society during the 1970s — a time of crisis of both economy and society. The United Kingdom had hardly adjusted to the loss of the empire when the question of membership in the European Economic Community (EEC) was put high on the agenda. The political pressures and the rapid economic decline led to an "identity crisis" of British society. "It was, in short, a crisis. Everybody said so, though perhaps it was just the crisis of capitalism. It was time for a change, though there was no unanimity about the direction, or the extent to which it would be choked by the conservatism which was a feature of twentieth-century British life. ... Could the cultural clock be turned back in order to preserve the future?" (Robbins 1985:292) Within the intelligentsia, which was very likely inspired by the processes of decolonization in the Third World, there was a growing concern that the centralizing and leveling tendencies of modern society were a threat to the existence of the small rural community and more generally to the rich diversity of local "cultures" in the British Isles. This concern has been fostered by, what Bell, Newby, Saunders and Rose (Bell et. al. 1978:56) have called "...the reassertion of a romantic anti-urbanism and anti-industrialism in Western societies during the early 1970s." Cohen has clearly shown, how the revival of community studies in British social anthropology related to the changing social climate in British society. In the second volume of the new series *Anthropological Studies of Britain*, he wrote, that the revival of interest in the anthropology of rural communities in Britain "... has also been prompted and provoked by a populist tendency to cultural 'localism' which has forced us to revise our over-simple view of the homogeneous nature of British culture, a caricature much exploited by politicians and the mass media, although thoroughly misleading and reviled by the members of localities, who see in it a gross misrepresentation of their special circumstances and of their distinctive cultures." (Cohen 1982b:1) When we look at Cohen's programmatic statement, it will be evident that the return to the study of indigenous cultures in the British Isles had a strong political background. Anthropologists were well aware that so many different cultures all over the world had been destroyed by political and/ or economic forces — the distinctive features of these cultures were dismissed as anachronistic and barbarous and declared to be an obstacle to modernization. Furthermore, they were also aware that the supposed cultural homogeneity of the modern nation-states (such as Britain) served the needs of the capitalist world economy. They were afraid that the "... 'centre' (the capital, Brussels, Wall Street, or wherever) ..." (Cohen

1986a:viii) would spread a homogeneous identity through fashion, mass production and mass media. A society that would be the product of those ideas was certainly not the kind of society they had envisioned. Anthropologists and, to a certain extent, the members of the communities concerned were afraid that the distinctiveness of the local community was threatened "... by the diminution of structural boundaries: geographical distance is bridged by improved transportation and communication; cultural distance is attacked by standardisation and the denigration of local difference by those at the centre." (Cohen 1986a:ix) Apparently, the threat to rural communities was not only an academic vision, it turned out to be a real one. In the rural areas of Britain the massive upheavals in the national and international political economy during the 1970s caused major changes in the economic system, the social relations and the political balance. Counterurbanization, decentralization of certain forms of industrial activities and infrastructure, and the growing industrialization of agriculture coincided with an extensive restructuring and centralization of rural administration. Local government was reorganized and after Britain became a member of the EEC agricultural, fishery and regional policies were absorbed into the EEC framework. As a result the "... loss of local accountability has increased political sensitivity of many rural issues." (Bradley & Lowe 1984:1) — The feeling of being under threat from the centre may have further increased in the 1980s because of, what Gareth Rees (1985:1) has called, the vengeance of the New Right in the shape of Mrs. Thatcher's Conservative governments. Its emphasis on individualism and policies which aimed at increasing the political control of the centre further undermined the role of collectivities.

As a consequence of the economic, political and social developments, the 1970s witnessed a change in the view of the United Kingdom held by various social "sciences". The research interest in locality and localism in rural communities came from two different directions: political economy and social anthropology. While political economy concentrated on "... the locality as the spatial focus for the reproduction of labour power within capitalist society ...", the social anthropologists, on the other hand, were more interested in "... the culture of localism and the identification with place ..." (Bradley & Lowe 1984:7). The renewed interest in locality was due to the review of the assumption that the United Kingdom is a homogeneous entity. In political science the United Kingdom had, until the 1960s, been accepted, "as a textbook example of a homogeneous society where influences and characteristics were equally significant and effective throughout the whole territory." (Urwin 1982:19) This assumption was thoroughly revised during the 1970s. For example, Michael Hechter's (1975) radical description of British centre-periphery relations in terms of internal colonialism — inspired by the theory of underdevelopment that was applied to Latin American countries (see Hechter 1975:30-34) — was widely discussed and contributed much to a revision of the "English" view of Britain as culturally homogeneous (which meant, of course, predominantly English) nation[19].

In social anthropology, Frankenberg's rural-urban continuum (see pages 18-26) provided an excellent example for the uncritical acceptance of the concept of Britain as a homogeneous society. The communities chosen by Frankenberg to represent certain stages on his rural-urban continuum were located throughout Britain and even in Ireland. A major flaw of his approach is the application of a single rural-urban continuum to culturally very diverse areas — Wales, Northern England, Southern England, the London area, and Ireland. This necessarily implies that there exists some kind of common overarching structure (Britain as a nation state), which imposes a certain degree of homogeneity, because a homogeneous framework is necessary to guarantee the comparability of these communities. To assume that, for example, the concept of class has the same implications in an English "truly rural" community as in a Welsh "truly rural" community may seem entirely reasonable because both the English and the Welsh community are part of the "British class system". However, I believe that the contrary is the case, the meaning of class in a Welsh rural community is to a large extent different from the meaning of class in an English rural community. In addition to that, there are differences in the distribution of classes throughout the United Kingdom. Placing both communities within a single (evolutionary) framework would, therefore, simply negate the different historical, political, and economic background, as well as the cultural differences between those two communities[20]. This is not to say, that local communities are not part of an overarching structure like the British nation state — I certainly do not want

---

19 For a description of Hechter's approach and the critique raised against it see pages 74-76.

20 The problem of class relations and the different meaning of class categories in Wales, and their relation to the wider British context, will be dicussed in the chapters 7-9.

to run the risk of being accused of naivety — however, a concept, like the rural-urban continuum, which levels cultural distinctiveness is of dubious value for the understanding of Britain as a whole. Only a framework which incorporates these differences can lead to a better understanding of both Britain as a multinational state and its culturally diverse parts (nations, regions and communities) — which are enclosed by the larger entity, while in some respects transcending it.

Fortunately, during the 1970s, the idea of the rural-urban continuum was dumped on the rubbish heap of futile attempts at grand sociological theorizing. While the rural-urban continuum was slowly decomposing, anthropologists were searching for a more productive way of thinking about their own society.

5 CULTURE, SYMBOLISM AND COMMUNITY

Interestingly, the critical introspection of social anthropologists turned out to be a return to the roots of modern anthropology. Anthropologists have turned full circle, back to the major interests of the nineteenth century: symbolism, ritual, and classification (Jackson 1987:8 and Kuper 1987:189). With the advent of post-modernist anthropology a paradigm shift occurred, in which, Cohen (1987:210) argued, the theoretical problem of the relationship of the individual to society as it related to the *explanation* of social organization, was gradually displaced by an increasing concern with the symbolization of culture. The so-called post-modernist anthropology was not interested in such an abstract issue as how society is structured, instead it concentrates on exploring people's experience of social interaction.

The return to the anthropology of "culture" and the interest in the symbolization of culture is evident in the work of Anthony P. Cohen — perhaps the most influential anthropologist of the community studies revival. Cohen is mainly concerned with the problem of how and why local communities, in times of severe threats to their structural boundaries by a powerful centre, which tries to impose its structures upon them, can maintain a sense of distinctiveness. Cohen assumed, that the members of communities have developed such a determined response to changes imposed from outside because the community provides a social space within which they can define their identity as individuals and as part of a collective. Thus, when the community is threatened with destruction, it members feel that an important part of their identity will also be destroyed. He argued that the community can maintain its distinctiveness, in spite of the destruction of many of its distinctive structural features, by *re*-constructing its boundaries symbolically. It is *re*-constructed symbolically by the members of the community through the internal discourse of the meaning of community, because symbols are flexible enough to allow for internal differences of meaning attached to them. Furthermore, the meaning of the symbols is not intelligible for the outside world, and thus not controllable or threatened by external forces.

Although, Cohen's approach to the study of rural communities in Britain is far from revolutionary, it is a practicable and useful way of gaining insights into the complex phenomenon of the reassertion of community in a constantly changing environment.

Like Arensberg and Kimball's community study method, Cohen's approach is basically empirical and inductive. The theory must be grounded in the data, and the method of data collection must be rooted in the social context from which the data are drawn. The emphasis lies on the anthropologists' comprehension of the members' perceptions of themselves and their symbolic construction of the community. Thus, the *reality* of the community is observable in the "social forms and cultural behaviour" (Arensberg & Kimball 1972:3) as a whole. "This task of assimilating the means by which the community is known to its members is, then, fundamental to the discovery of its dynamics, its culture, whose description is the real business of the ethnographer." (Cohen 1978:12)

Although some of the basic assumptions of Cohen's and Arensberg and Kimball's approaches to the study of the community appear to be consonant, Cohen does not strive for the ultimate theory explaining the evolution of human communities. He abandoned the idea of grand sociological theory and argued for grounded theory instead. The application of grand sociological theory would mean that the anthropologist would drown local distinctiveness in the sea of universal laws, he/she would transform difference into likeness, and thereby prevent the comprehension of the distinctive features of the culture he studied. "That is a procedure which would seem to be totally at odds with the comprehension of culturally discrete milieux whose distinctiveness from the metropolitan mass is both a function of their relative isolation and is also a raison d'être for their continued survival." (Cohen 1978:7-8) The preoccupation of anthropologists and sociologists with structure has only revealed the common mask of the community — which conceals internal variety and presents the community as a coherent entity to the outside world — and mistaken it for "objective" form. The community is more complex than the so-called objective forms elicited by anthropological analysis make us believe. Cohen argued that community can no longer be adequately described in terms of structure and components, for it is a symbol to which its different individual members impute their own meanings (Cohen 1985a:74). Nevertheless, Cohen (1985a:98) had to admit that meaning is ethnographically problematic. It is impossible to achieve an objective description of meaning because it is only susceptible to interpretation and all we can aspire to is "informed speculation" (Cohen) or "insight" (cf. Leach 1986:52-53) — insight, however, is quite an achievement. "The issue now is not how to construct a 'scientific' explanation, nor even how to reconcile the observer's science with the subject's behaviour; it is, rather, one of how to achieve an understanding of a social situation which most nearly comprehends the understanding its members have of it." (Cohen 1978:4-5)

Nevertheless, he was also aware of the problems involved in the use of the concept community by its members. The idea of community expressed by its members is only a partial idea, actually generated through their experience of sectional interest and segmentary membership. Thus, he argued, that we have to be aware of the fact that the uncritical reproduction of the people's idea of community would "... give quality of authority and objectivity to a partial idea. ... 'The community' may be a generalisation from these partial views; or it may be a way of emphasising their discreteness. In either case 'the community' is seen through the medium of its parts." (Cohen 1987:59-60) However, he assumed that, when we study a community, we must study it as a whole because the constituent parts can only be understood in reference to the construct of the whole (Cohen 1978:13). Cohen's experience with the segments of the Shetland Island community of Whalsay showed that the community and its constituting segments stood in a dialectical relationship to each other (Cohen 1987:59). His concept of the whole corresponds with Durkheim's idea that the whole is greater than the sum of its parts which take their character from it (Cohen 1985a:116). The problem of this holistic approach is that the whole can only be approached through its parts. Therefore, Cohen (1978:16) argued that the anthropologist, in order to achieve an appropriate understanding of the field, should make sense of the parts by locating and constructing them in the same way as his subjects. For Cohen the use of the concept of community was not an "unjustifiable reification" of a misleading ideal. He claimed that the use of the concept is justifiable because the people speak of community as an entity which has some independent existence imputed to it. Community is "... that social and spatial entity which forms the basic environment for *Ego's* social relations, which provide him with the rules of behaviour, which gives him means of valuing, understanding, knowing, expressing and so forth." (Cohen 1978:13) It is not just constructed in terms of locality but more appropriately in terms of a primacy of belonging because it is the entity which is more meaningful and emotionally binding than "... the abstraction we call 'society'." (Cohen 1985a:15) Cohen assumed that the unit of study, the local community, must be conceived as a coherent and self-consciously distinctive *cultural* entity (Cohen 1978:19). He defined this cultural entity as the *real community*, and — referring to Arensberg and Kimball's concept — saw it as *a master social system* (Cohen 1978:2, footnote 1)[21]. Communities are *real* in the sense that they recognize themselves as distinctive, and reiterate this distinctiveness through the continuous operation and elaboration of *culture*.

To define culture, Cohen used Geertz's definition. Geertz believed "... that man is an animal suspended in webs of significance he himself has spun ...", and he took culture to be those webs (Geertz 1973:5). Cohen (1985a:17) found three principles in Geertz's concept of culture that were important for his approach. Firstly, culture is "... continually created and recreated by people through their social interaction, rather than imposed upon them ..."; and secondly it has "...neither deterministic power nor objectively identifiable referents... "; and finally it is manifest "...in the capacity with which it endows people to perceive meaning in, or to attach meaning to social behaviour." It was especially the processual nature of Geertz's concept which appealed to Cohen. He argued (1985a:16-17) that because people's understanding of their community resides in their orientation to its symbolism, the relations between symbolism, culture and meaning are crucial for the analysis of the concept of community. The Community is important for the individual because within the confines of the community he/she acquires culture, which means, he/she learns to make sense of the symbolic equipment of its culture — he/she learns to make meaning. Consequently, Cohen assumed, that we make sense of behaviour by an act of interpretation since the behaviour which we have observed does not have an inherent meaning. When we interact, we thus make and act upon interpretations of behaviour. Social interaction, based on interpretation, implies a certain degree of subjectivity which suggests

---

21 For Arensberg and Kimball's definition see page 13.

the possibility of imprecision, ambiguity and idiosyncracy. Although the interpretations of the same event are likely to differ for different people, they may not be aware of this difference. Their disagreement is, therefore, not necessarily an obstacle for their successful interaction; on the contrary, people can often find common ground whilst preserving their own subjective interpretations. However, these interpretations are neither random nor immutable, for they tend to be made in terms characteristic of a given society. They are influenced by language, ecology, traditional beliefs and ideology, etc., and are responsive to circumstances of interaction (Cohen 1985a:17).

Distinctiveness, the perception and construction of difference, is one of the key concepts in Cohen's approach to the study of the community. "The ethnography of the locality is an account of how people experience and express their difference from others, and of how their sense of difference becomes incorporated into and informs the nature of their social organization and process." (Cohen 1982a:2) Therefore, Cohen did not attempt another definition of community but started off by seeking a "reasonable interpretation" of the usage of the word community — he turned to praxis instead of theory. The word's use implies basically two related suggestions: that members of a group have something in common, and that this distinguishes them from members of other groups. Community is, thus, a relational idea — implying both similarity and difference — which is constituted in opposition to other communities or other social entities. He argued, that "... the use of the word is only occasioned by the desire or need to express such a distinction ..." and that "... the element which embodies this sense of discrimination ..." is the boundary.

The concept of the process of boundary construction is similar to Fredrik Barth's concept of the boundaries of ethnic groups. According to Barth (1969:9-10) boundaries persist despite interaction and the flow of personnel across them, and important social relations are frequently based precisely on the distinction between the status of a member and the status of a non-member. "In other words, ethnic distinctions do not depend on an absence of social interaction and acceptance, but are quite contrary often the very foundations on which embracing social systems are built. Interaction in such a social system does not lead to its liquidation through change and acculturation; cultural differences can persist despite inter-ethnic contact and interdependence." (Barth 1969:10) This is especially relevant because in modern industrialized societies — which today means everywhere in the world — a community cannot exist in total isolation. Moreover, it is intertwined with the complex national and international economic, political, and social networks. But there is yet another, and crucial, aspect to the concept of the boundary: it is the dialectical process through which the boundary is created by the community and the community in turn is created by the boundary. The boundary encloses the identity of the community and its culture (Cohen 1985a:12); people become aware of their culture when they stand at its boundary — that means, when they interact across it. It is this process of interaction, the encounter with our own normative boundaries, which makes us aware of the distinctiveness and circumscription of our own behaviour (Cohen 1982b:4). Creation and maintenance of boundaries is not simply a process of becoming aware of one's own culture and community but also of attributing value to it, and, thereby, to others on the other side of the boundary. But under modern circumstances the former referents — locality, generation, class and gender — seem to have been transformed by forces of change emanating from the centre, that attack the structural boundaries (the markers of local distinctiveness) of the community and try to replace the structural basis of local diversity with a veneer of homogeneity (Cohen 1986b:1). Nevertheless, for most people the sense of difference has not disappeared, it has changed into a sense of difference not clearly expressed in structure. We should not be fooled by a similarity of structure, for the response to the irreversible changes of the structure may be found in the different meanings attached to the structure and in the symbolic expression of this difference. Cohen said that we should not confuse the increasing similarities in the structure of people's lives with their response to it, for the response, the interpretation and attachment of meaning, is neither mechanical, nor necessarily overt: it is symbolic. "It is in the symbolic that we now look for people's sense of difference, and in symbolism, rather than structure, that we seek the boundaries of their worlds of identity and diversity." (Cohen 1986b:2)

Symbols are the vehicles of such interpretations, they make experience and meaning sharable but not identical. "Thanks to symbols, cultural meanings are rich, deep, multivocal, many layered, highly wrought, and shared but also rarified, subject to abstraction, exportable, often communicated: thus not substantially shared but rather *exchanged.*" (Boon 1982:121) According to Boon, symbols have not only the capacity to allow meanings to be exchanged, they also make experience paradoxical — the, presumably, same stimulus leads to variable cultural responses.

"Cultural symbols reveal a literal duplicity: (1) they mesh the options and possibilities (both real and imaginary) provided for in social action with the intellectual schemes that both guide and respond to action; thus they weave, interrelate, and cross-reference diverse spheres of life in society: cultural symbols integrate; *and* (2) they establish formulas that remain internally consistent regardless of context; without such formulas there could be no communication across cultures, no relative abstraction of one culture by another, no self-stereotyping by one culture against its stereotypes of others and, heaven forbid, no anthropology. Thus cultural symbols differentiate, indeed, sometimes alienate, the very integrities they integrate." (Ibid.)

Cohen (1985a:18, 1986b:9) argued that the flexibility of symbols allows the individual to experience and express his attachment to community without compromising his individuality. The community itself, and everything material as well as conceptual within it, has a symbolic dimension (Cohen 1985a:19). This dimension is not some kind of consensus of sentiment but, rather, it provides the individual with a means to make and to express meaning. Although the members of a community may all agree that they, as a collective, are different from other communities, they may also construct the meaning of these supposed quintessential differences in very different ways (Cohen 1986b:11). The community is, thus, not a uniform entity, however coherent it may appear at its boundary. It conceals variety, the difference of meaning attached to the boundary internally, behind a common set of symbols. The community, constituted by symbols, does not determine that all its members should make the same sense of the world, and if its members make similar sense of the world, it is because they are using the same set of symbols. The community aggregates individualities and provides the ranges within which individuality is recognizable — individuality and community are therefore reconcilable. In the process of the symbolic construction of community the reality of difference is continuously transformed into an appearance of similarity "... with such efficacy that people can still invest the 'community' with ideological integrity." (Cohen 1985a:21) In the process of uniting the members of the community in their opposition both to each other and to those outside it constitutes the community's boundaries. Thus, the community boundary is not drawn at the point where differentiation occurs, but it incorporates and encloses differences and is thereby strengthened (Cohen 1986b:13). The construction of boundaries from the distinctive meanings present in the community's social discourse is a dialectical process. It provides the individual with important referents for his own identity, while, at the same time, expressing and reinforcing the boundary through the presentation of those identities in social life (Cohen 1985a:117).

For its members the community has two faces, a *public face* turned to the outside world and a *private face* that is only visible to them. The public face, or the "typical mode", is a mask or a stereotype behind which the internal variety disappears or coalesces into a simple symbolic statement. The private face, or the "idiosyncratic mode", on the other hand, does not conceal the internal variety. Behind it, through the process of internal discourse, differentiation, variety and complexity proliferate and generate a complex symbolic statement that is only intelligible for members of the community (Cohen 1986b:13, 1985a:74). Anthropologists should be pri-

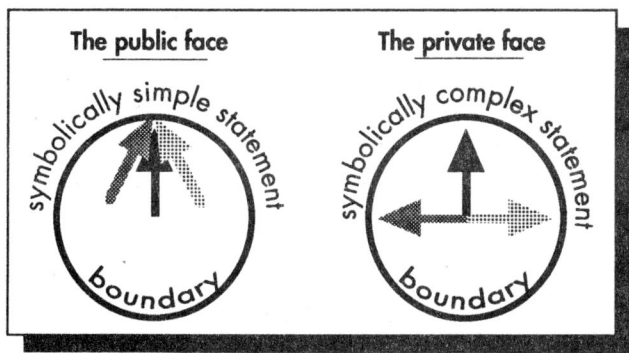

Fig. 2 The two faces of the community boundary (cf. Cohen 1985a:74).

marily concerned with the idiosyncratic mode, "... for it is here that we encounter people thinking about symbolizing their community. It is in these depths of 'thinking', rather than in the surface appearance of 'doing' that culture is to be sought." (Cohen 1985a:75)

The symbolic aspect of the boundary — the meaning given to it by the people — is, therefore, crucial for the understanding of the importance of the community in people's experience. Through the symbolic construction, or should we say *re*-construction, of the boundary, the community has found a way to maintain its distinctiveness despite the destruction of its structural defences (Cohen 1987:11). But why should the people want to preserve their distinctiveness, their community? Cohen showed that for the inhabitants of Whalsay the community is a reality that hinges crucially on consciousness, for it is "... invested with all the sentiments attached to kinship, friendship, neighbouring, familiarity, jealousy, as they inform the social process of everyday life." (Cohen 1985a:13) The community is a symbolic construct that each member can invest with his self, without overly compromising his identity. "Indeed the gloss of communality which it paints over the diverse components gives each of them an additional referent for their identity." (Cohen 1985a:109) The vehemence of its response to the encroachment of its boundaries, is due to its members feeling that because the community is threatened with destruction, they themselves will go down with it. This feeling is deeply rooted in the dialectical relationship of individual and community. To its members the community is an agglomerate informed by their individual personalities. On the other hand, the community also gives them the means to "... find their identity as individuals through their occupancy of the community's social space: if outsiders trespass in that space, then its occupants' own sense of self is felt to be debased and defaced." (Ibid.) Identity is always tenuous when the physical and structural boundaries of the community are increasingly blurred. In such circumstances the community can be easily depicted as being threatened by some external source and, therefore, can become a means for mobilizing collectivity. Thus implicit or explicit contrast is crucial for the perception of a sense of social self at the level of both individuality and collectivity. Cohen argued, that the vitality of cultures lies in their juxtaposition — they exaggerate themselves and others — and that "culture is thus inherently antithetical". Further, the contrasts made by a culture are symbolic — they lack fixed "objective" meanings — and therefore contingent and relational (Cohen 1985a:115).

As we have seen, the consciousness of the community is encapsulated in the perception of its boundaries which are symbolically constructed by the interaction. Thus, the boundaries of a community are categories of social knowledge marked by symbolism. Cohen argued that social change through modernization may enhance the salience of symbolism. The imposition of our meaning on the behaviour of other people may provoke them to insist on the uniqueness, integrity or distinctiveness of their behaviour. It seems to be this mechanism which leads communities and ethnic groups to the reassertion or reaffirmation of their boundaries. Such assertiveness is likely to intensify as the conceived similarity between forms or structures on each side of the boundary increases (Cohen 1985a:40). Cohen encountered the process of growing consciousness and reinforcement of the boundary by means of cultural symbolism in the Shetland island community of Whalsay which experienced intensive social change. "In an atmosphere of such boundary consciousness, almost any behaviour, however pragmatic, can be made grist to the mill of cultural symbolism." (Cohen 1985b:308)

Modernization involves the importation of alien structural forms across the community boundaries, which, in turn, threaten to replace the structural basis of the boundary. The fact that alien structural forms are imported, does not necessarily mean that they can also transfer their meaning unchanged and impose it upon the members of the community. Nevertheless, many community sociologists and anthropologists believed in the myth that the cultural imperialism of the centre (the nation state) would transform the rural community into an image of the centre. But conformity is often an illusion because the externally imposed forms will be transformed by the members of a community into "... an idiom more consonant with indigenous culture." (Cohen 1985a:36) They may substitute the external meanings with their own meanings and use them to serve their own symbolic purposes. It may seem ironic, but the new external forms may well become media for the reassertion and symbolic expression of the community boundary. As a result, the community boundary will become a more symbolic, more mental construct while the physical and geographical aspects of the boundary become less important. However, not only external forms will be transformed in the process of the symbolic expression of community. Traditional forms which have lost their structural significance, are invested with new meanings as a result of, or response to, social change. Being aware of the threat to the integrity of the community as a discrete entity, the members mobilize their cultural and symbolic reserves to create and assert a sense of distinctiveness which is consonant with their changed situation. The meaning of old forms is transformed by the contrivance of new meanings which are largely imperceptible for the outside world. "Through such counterpunching the apparent homogeneity of the 'modern' society supposedly creeping out from the Centre and insinuating itself into the nooks and crannies of the margin is revealed as a somewhat superficial veneer. Moreover, it is a veneer which, ironically protects the vitality of the margin and enables it to nurture its new distinguishing features while concealed from the maw of the Centre's cultural imperialism." (Cohen 1985b:320) Thus, the community is symbolically constituted through the process of deploying, interpreting and transforming symbols. The symbolic boundary may be very difficult, if not impossible, to recognize for non-members. This is an important factor for the survival of the community as a distinctive entity, because the efficacy of the process of symbolic boundary construction and maintenance depends on the outside world being unable to recognize the boundary at all, or recognize it in those terms in which it is defined through the internal discourse (Cohen 1985b:309). "The distance between centre and periphery, between bounded community and the outside world, is now often of this conceptual variety. Indeed, the conceptual distance is elaborated and embellished to maintain the authentic distinctiveness of the community." (Cohen 1985a:37)

History (myth) and ritual play important roles as symbolic devices through which the authentic distinctiveness of the community is maintained — they heighten consciousness of the community and strengthen its boundaries.

Through rituals people experience community, because they confirm and strengthen their social identity and the sense of social location. Furthermore, they can serve to symbolize the character of the community as a whole in opposition to other groups, and provide the members of the community with acceptable terms of reference in which to express and evaluate their personal identities (Cohen 1985a:50-57). "The 'community', in this regard, is a cluster of symbolic and ideological map references with which the individual is socially oriented." (Cohen 1985a:57) Cohen argued, that it is the very nature of symbolism that it provides not only the means for discrimination, but that it also implies a sense of negation. In that sense, rituals can not only serve to mark boundaries but also to negate the norms of behaviour and values which normally define them. However, the ritualized inversion or negation of the norm — the symbolic reversal of normality — emphasizes and reasserts the norm by implicitly marking the prevailing social order in contradistinction to others; thereby, it ensures the continuity of the community. "The inversion of the norm is not only limited to ritual, but may be found also in all manner of symbolic forms. For example, an increasingly common response to the imposition of stigmatic identity appears to be an assertion by those stigmatized of the characteristics which 'spoil' their identity ... rather than to mask them." (Cohen 1985a:59) This tendency to destigmatize the stigma, by rendering it as a positive value, is a recent strategy of ethnic and other disadvantaged groups. In the process of inverting the stigma "...the disadvantaged group rejects the symbolic code in which it is disadvantaged, and replaces it by its own in which it is relatively powerful or to which it has exclusive access." (Cohen 1985a:60) This rejection and replacement of the majority's symbolic code — what Cohen, referring to Schwimmer, called symbolic competition — re-establishes the feeling of superiority of the minority group which will in reality remain in the position of a oppressed minority. In short, the symbolic reversal of normality can be employed, firstly, to emphasize and reassert the norm and, secondly, to reject the norm and to replace it by another (Cohen 1985a:63).

Furthermore, there is a third form of symbolic reversal which combines both forms. The symbolic world created by this kind of symbolic reversal is "... a kind of fantastic reconstruction of empirical society: the dialectical contrast between the two is resolved by a reassertion of the inevitability and desirability of the first through recognition of the fantasy and impossibility of the second." (Cohen 1985a:63) In the sense that symbolism and ritual are mechanisms which bridge the gap between ideal (belief) and actual (reality), this fantasy is also a way to manage change without a severe disruption of the familiar concepts of community. The fantasy permits the customary symbolic form to be used in radically changed circumstances, and, thereby, enables the members of the community to make sense of these circumstances through the use of familiar idioms (Cohen 1985a:92).

These familiar idioms refer to a past or a tradition which is believed to be threatened by contemporary circumstances. It may seem paradoxical that the re-assertion of community is achieved through exactly those idioms which are supposed to be replaced by these circumstances. In the process of symbolically expressing the community, the past is used as a resource. History is a selective construction of the past which reflects present circumstances. Cohen compared folk history to myth, which he defined as an "... expression of the way people cognitively map past, present and future. In the struggle to interpret, we use our past experience to render stimuli into a form sufficiently familiar that we can attach some sense to them." (Cohen 1985a:99) Through our past experiences we make the present intelligible — past experiences serve as a model of reality, a framework for interpretation. Both individuals and collectivities refer to such cognitive maps to orient themselves in interaction. The past, or history, used in this process is constructed according to the requirements of the present; it can never be a fact in itself. In everyday discourse symbols of the past are condensed to simple historical labels. An example for this kind of discourse is the use of the simplistic artifice of 'Victorian values' by Margaret Thatcher and the Conservative Party, who used them "... to lend credence and ethical validity to economic monetarianism." (Cohen 1985a:101-102) This emblematic use of Queen Victoria is precisely such a condensation of a more complicated story into a simple historical label; it is a mnemonic form. Referring to Turner, Cohen called these forms 'condensation symbols'. The use of such symbols triggers an emotional response. Norms and values will be charged with emotions and basic emotions will become ennobled in conjunction with them. "Symbols of the 'past', mythically infused with timelessness, have precisely this competence, and attain particular effectiveness during periods of intensive social change when communities have to drop their heaviest cultural anchors in order to resist the currents of transformation." (Cohen 1985a:102)

However, not all communities have developed a determined and vibrant response to change. Cohen assumed that the consciousness of difference and the determined re-assertion of community is a universal feature of peripheral communities. Those peripheral communities often are — and/or see themselves as — marginal to the political and social context of the nation state. "Peripherality, marginality, can be collective self-images, informing and informed by a community's perception of its inability to affect the course of events — even to affect its own destiny." (Cohen 1982b:6) This sense of disadvantage or subordination, however, does not necessarily imply the re-assertion of cultural integrity. The question, we must ask, is: what produces such vehemence and assertiveness in some groups? Cohen (1985a:104) believed that "... the most instructive precedents relate to the political assertion of cultural difference — a phenomenon generally described through the somewhat abused label of 'ethnicity'." He criticized the "over-theorized" (Cohen 1985a:106) attempts to distinguish between different kinds of collective sentiments (be they ethnic, national, or whatever), for they do not provide insights into the people's inclination to give preference to their community membership over their higher scale attachments. Instead, Cohen (1985a:107) proposed a shift in focus from the causes of ethnicity to some form of sub-national communal sentiment which would make a relevant contribution to the "ethnicity debate" possible. The question which could be taken to the field, would be the question of why the idiom of communal sentiment sometimes stresses the ethnic, and sometimes a different sectionalism. "Ethnicity, couched in the rhetoric of kinship, implies a degree of communality sufficiently high to override intervening sectional interests in given situations. This communality becomes increasingly persuasive since the 'higher level' claims of its obsolescence are manifestly unwarranted. It is a convincing level of sociality to contrast with the national and supra-national entities which are recognized increasingly as having failed to deliver economic and political goods. This failure itself breeds another: the bankruptcy of the higher level entities as socio-psychological repositories of identity." Cohen suggested that the assertion or re-assertion of community, whether ethnic or local, could be due to the recognition of community as the most adequate medium for the collective expression of each member's whole self. This does not imply, however, that the members of a communal group necessarily perceive an identity of interest between themselves and their community — it could simply provide them with a model for the political formulation of their interests and aspirations. On the other hand, community could also provide not so much a model, but more an advantageous medium for the expression of the diverse interests and aspirations of its members.

We should, therefore, treat the transitions from *Gemeinschaft* to *Gesellschaft*, organic solidarity to mechanical solidarity, status to contract not so much as theories of social change rendering the community obsolete, but as coexisting modalities of behaviour within any society at any given time (Cohen 1985a:116). In treating the contrasting states as coexistent, we will be able to see the (*re-*)assertion of community not as an abnormal phenomenon to be explained, but as a normal expression of resilience of culture. "The process may be anathema to some powerful forces in modern society; but that may be to say only that it calls now to a greater extend than in the past on that sense of self and the ingenuity with which it may be expressed. Community, whether local or ethnic, or in whatever form, need not therefore be seen as an anachronism in urban-industrial society. Rather it should be regarded as one of the modalities of behaviour available within such societies. That its symbolic expression is frequently in terms antagonistic to the larger society is a matter of interest, but not of pathology." (Cohen 1985a:117)

6 COMMUNITY STUDIES IN THE 1980s

TOWARDS A NEW SOCIAL ANTHROPOLOGY OF BRITAIN?

Apparently, a determined group of social anthropologists has saved the locality focused "community study" from falling into oblivion. However, the emphasis on the interpretation of symbolism, the importance of boundaries, the subjects' perceptions of themselves and their symbolic construction of community, hermeneutic rather than positivistic concepts, were not really new concepts in British social anthropology. Their application to the study of indigenous cultures in the British Isles has nevertheless produced some new and valuable insights. Whether it is a *powerful new wave* in social anthropology that will lead to a *new* British ethnography, however, is still an open question[22]. The community studies revival was part of a paradigm shift in anthropology, but it was not a driving force behind it. This paradigm shift was partly the result of the debate about the usefulness and ethics of anthropology, which was caused by a increasingly self-conscious rejection of anthropology by the now indigenous governments of the ex-colonies. Anthropologists realized that the relations between the different constituent parts of the United Kingdom were not so different from the relations between the United Kingdom and its oversees colonies. "In each case (in the colonial world, in the contemporary Third World, and in that Europe which anthropologists study) we find what may be termed 'disjunctive' social, political, and economic systems. Often over a long period, previously disparate formations have been conjoined, with varying degrees of tightness and looseness, as a roughly connected system. The process of connection itself generates various kinds of differentiation and difference between and within the constituent elements. Relations of

---

22 *Symbolising Boundaries*, the second volume in the series *Anthropological Studies of Britain*, was advertised as presenting case studies that "belong to the powerful new wave in social anthropology which has been called the 'new British ethnography'." (See back cover of Cohen 1986a)

centrality and peripherality are created, with those at the margin having problems – or indeed being themselves seen as problems – for which plans and policies are required. What seem to be gaps appear, and it is in those gaps that we find the anthropologist." (Grillo 1985:18) Consequently, anthropologists felt that it was not a mere academic question, but an issue of great political importance, whether or not the distinctive local cultures of British communities could survive the onslaught of the national and international centres. In contrast to planners and politicians who may assume that the local community is an obsolete relic of the past within a modern industrial economy, "... anthropology as a discipline tends to take an activist, and perhaps at times naively optimistic, stance in defence of cultural survival. Indeed, Bruner suggests that this — the face of localism as resistance — is the current ethnographic paradigm of cultural representation (1986)." (Nadel-Klein 1991:514)

In contrast to Boissevain (1975) who was inspired by the world-system perspective of development anthropology, and consequently called for a move beyond the community — he envisaged a social anthropology of Europe that could be called an "anthropology of national and supranational processes" (Boissevain 1975:16) — social anthropology had returned to the anthropology of cultural processes at "community" level. That is not to say, that social anthropologists were not concerned with British society as a whole. Strathern, for example, argued that we can learn from the particular case of Elmdon something about English society as a whole and, furthermore, that we can only make sense of the village situation by considering it in terms of certain general principles. Nevertheless, she was also aware of the inherent danger of generalizations. "The danger, of course, is that the account will hop from the particular Elmdon incident which illuminates the 'general' feature to filling patchy village data with what we all imagine English kinship is about. I make no further apology for this. If I slide between frames of reference it is because I am in pursuit less of sociological explanation than of conceptual insights. Indeed, to appreciate the force of ideas and concepts one may have to jump context. The particular case is both contained within and distinct from general characteristics of English kinship, as Elmdon village is both a part of English society and a unique manifestation of certain select elements. How far it is 'typical' puts the question the wrong way. Any understanding to be gained from detailed study must face both directions: as at one and the same time an example of the workings out of principles which illuminates the general case, and equally an example only of itself, largely non-replicable." (Strathern 1982a:78)

Cohen has also quite clearly shown that the vehement re-assertion of communal identity is part of the processes of social change which affect the whole of modern British society. The new framework developed for the analysis of local communities was more consonant with the diversity of cultures in the British Isles than the previous attempts at grand sociological theory had been (for example the rural-urban continuum). However, the concept of the symbolic construction of community has been criticized by sociologists (Day & Murdoch 1993) and anthropologists (Nadel-Klein 1991) alike for being too preoccupied with the inside view of the local construction of community and losing sight of the wider social, political and economic context. Day and Murdoch (1993:92-93) believe that the progress for understanding the symbolic construction of community had been achieved at the expense of ignoring the problem of the spatiality of social relationships. They argue that the institutional context was not sufficiently explored in the analyses, and that people's experience and expression of difference is closely connected with the institutions of which people are a part; how these institutions structure, and are themselves structured by, the experience of locality and community. The salience of community, so they argue, becomes manifest at the interface between local and external institutions and through participation in "key" institutions the members of a community can bring about or resist change. The reason for the importance of institutions lies in the fact that "... actors, operating within institutions, attempt to maintain and develop both their own identities, and the social settings within which such identities can be expressed." Their assumptions should be viewed with caution because they are based on data from 38 unstructured interviews, with what they called (Day & Murdoch 1993:95, footnote 1) "... key respondents, such as local councillors, business people and those involved in running village organizations ...", and a survey of 30% of the households in their research area (Upper Ithon valley, Powys). It is, therefore, not surprising that they stress the importance of institutions in the process of the construction of community. However, the stress on the institutional frame is misleading in the sense that internal diversity is reduced to the public face of the community's boundary which is created in their so-called "key institutions". In focusing on a specially selected number of "key" informants, the representation of the community created by one segment is mistaken for notions of community and locality which are the product of the process of interaction between actors within a variety of social, political and economic networks (Day & Murdoch 1993:109).

Jane Nadel-Klein[23] (1991:501) criticized the so-called "new British ethnography", and in particular Anthony P. Cohen, for not going "... far enough in exploring localism as a product of modern political economy." She argued (Ibid.:502) "... that historically, the global division of labor has alternately produced and then marginalized localism as an integral part of the process and the cultural construction of class." She therefore suggested (Nadel-Klein 1991:501-502) that "... a complementary approach to understanding the persistent power of localism is to ask how 'localism' has actually become a virtual synonym for 'marginality'." Her idea of the relevance of anthropology corresponds partly with Boissevain's concept for an anthropology of national and supra-national processes. Like Boissevain (1975:14), she is concerned with the transfer of power from the local community to the national and international political apparatus and the subsequent reduction of local autonomy. Understanding localism and the production of marginality in Europe as an integral part of the global division of labour, may make the connection and the processes of power distribution between the so-called First and Third/Fourth World clearer (Nadel-Klein 1991:514). However, Nadel-Klein's assessment of the relevance of European anthropology for the understanding of global processes is certainly more refined than Boissevain's. For Boissevain, doing anthropology in Europe should provide a remedy for the ex-colonial states who also faced the innumerable "... izations" — industrialization, urbanization, centralization, bureaucratization, etc. — so that we can spare them from the often unintended consequences these processes have for small communities (Boissevain 1975:12). In other words, anthropology was seen as a way to pay off the debts of colonialism. Although this is believed to be a noble task, it may also turn out to be only a kind of intellectual neocolonialism[24] (cf. Leach 1986:49-50; Grillo 1985); its pur-

---

23 She has undertaken fieldwork (1975 and 1984) in the Scottish east coast village of Ferryden and the town of Montrose to investigate the impact of North Sea oil development upon social identity and political power in Scotland (Nadel-Klein 1991:500)

24 Interestingly, the vast majority of anthropologists who wanted to rescue the cultural distinctiveness of the *Celtic Fringe* from the iron grip of the Centre came from the *English Centre* (cf. Grillo 1985:16).

pose being the satisfaction of, what Sandra Wallman (cited by Grillo 1985:28) has called, "a chronic desire to be useful". Furthermore, Boissevain also indulged in the illusory view of social anthropology as a social *science* (for the science-art controversy see also pp. 20-25). He claimed, that the aim of social anthropology "... is to gain insights into social relations and processes in order to *explain* the past, understand the present and predict the future." (Boissevain 1975:12, emphasis added) I believe that the problem of the predictability of future developments is very closely connected with the desire to be useful, for the predictability of social development seems to be a prerequisite for the so-called usefulness to society. British social anthropology, however, was quite content with trying to understand a small part of the present and left the prediction of the future to those who claimed to be experts at it: soothsayers and magicians.

Nadel-Klein's approach is also firmly rooted in the present. During her study of Ferryden and Montrose she discovered an important difference in the use of the idiom of localism that was connected with class differences. Like Cohen, she saw the pervasiveness of localism or community identity as a form of resistance, but she also believed (Nadel-Klein 1991:510) that the process of symbolic maintenance of the community could not be understood "... without its complementary oppositional face: the views of the 'upper classes,' or those who act locally but who proclaim localism to be provincial and inferior and who characterize the villagers as 'other'." She argued that, even though the regional elites of North Angus denied that localism was relevant for their own sense of identity, they relied on it to construct class boundaries, and, furthermore, "... that their denigration of localism may reflect new uncertainties about the social content of class in Britain today, particularly with respect to the notion of a gentry." Due to the post-war and post-oil boom economic changes, the upper class of the county was divided into two groups, which were nevertheless increasingly overlapping. Those two groups were the gentry, the landowning elite who descended form the eighteenth century lairds, and the new elite of prosperous merchants and farmers. Despite the fact that the entrepreneurial groups have challenged the boundaries of the upper class, the distinctions of prestige and authority have persisted. Kinship plays a crucial role for the construction of the group's boundary. The group relations within the upper class are conceptualized in terms of kinship. "Successful farmers who lack the proper social and kinship credentials, despite their wealth and their presence on corporate boards, are not fully accepted by the heirs to 18th century privilege." (Ibid.:511) Nadel-Klein argued that the members of the upper class expressed two contradictory ideas, whose coexistence was made possible by the mediating factor of localism — on the one hand, they said that nobody cared about social class any longer because education and mobility have eradicated the distinctions; on the other hand, they claimed that class was of paramount importance because the "provincial" villagers continued to value hierarchy and deference. "For the gentry, and increasingly for the nouveaux riches, localism is a concept employed to distinguish themselves socially and culturally from the working and middle classes. They tend to regard local identity either as a quaint and primordial survival cherished mainly by the provincial and undereducated villagers or as an obsolete and regressive claim that impedes social improvement and economic development. While the gentry themselves may acknowledge a sense of having roots in a particular place, they also assert their freedom from that place through their extended supralocal (even international) networks." (Ibid.:513) Nadel-Klein concluded that the rejection of localism by the upper class can be usefully regarded as an objectified instrument of power. The geographically mobile and Anglicized upper class denied the validity of local voices by affirming their greater understanding of world affairs (especially economic affairs). As long as local identity was only quaint it could be tolerated or even manipulated for public relations, when it turned into resistance (for example, the objections to the oil base in Ferryden), however, tolerance was quickly forgotten. Anthropologists should not forget that the loss of cultural integrity for powerless groups is a process that not only dispossessed tribespeople of the Third World are facing — many groups in the so-called First World are also threatened. "For those without political power, cultural pride may be the only significant possession, indeed the only resource for resisting elite hegemony. While community identity is not a commodity that can be measured in the marketplace, the struggle for its possession is part of the political economy of change." (Ibid.:514-515)

The fact that the meaning attached to localism can vary with the different social horizon of those who attach meaning to it, was also shown by Marilyn Strathern in account of the Essex village of Elmdon. She argued that whatever their frames of reference, the use of localism draws attention to the boundedness of people's horizons. Localism conjures up several related images: being rooted in a place, the identity that comes from belonging, and a sense of antiquity and continuity over time. Moreover, every element of such imagery is contextualized by other ideas, rootedness by being rootless, belonging by the possibility not to belong, and the boundary by what lies beyond its confines. Thus, when each concept contains an inherent antithesis, we must construct the idea of local attachment in relation to the consequences of detachment (Strathern 1984:48). The idea of the boundedness of the local community also suggests that the boundary can be crossed. The notion of localism refers not only to the value of being local, it also refers to the value of mobility. Strathern believed that the village with a stable core and its outsiders, is a myth that will vanish under close anthropological scrutiny — the core disintegrates, the boundary appears permeable, and continuity seems disrupted. However, these ideas belong to the same set of cultural ideas which project the stable core. Strathern argued that belonging to a place and escaping from it, being at the same time fixed and mobile, is a model of class formation — a way in which class itself is thought about. "Indeed, since the formation of class society as we know it, I would suspect it has not been simply the 'village of the mind' that has had such salience but the 'vanishing village' of the mind." (Strathern 1984:48) Elmdon presents a paradox because one set of residents claimed that they belong, they said that they were the 'real' Elmdoners, and another set was very interested in claiming that they did not belong. Paradoxically both sets overlapped and depending on context some people claimed both. The claim of not being bounded by the village was important for claims of status which could not be obtained in the village. Especially for local women in Elmdon, kinship[25] provided a critical source of discrimination because through kinship they could lay claim to sources of status not otherwise apparent through the tracing of links outside the immediate family. "The idea of a fixed place, a locality, and of the possibility of moving between localities, constitute a complementary symbolic resource"; it is a demonstration of mobility in contradistinction to one's present fixture (Ibid.:49-50). Mobility is a key element in the English concept of status formation in which "... society is simultaneously composed of fixed strata and mobile individuals. 'Society' is thus separated from the 'persons' who compose it, and each entity is given a different value, in the same way as 'labour' is separated from the 'person' who activates it, each again being given a different value. These conceptualizations produce the distinctive postulate of class society that

---

25 In *Kinship at the Core*, Strathern (1981:169) has shown that kinship is the idiom which is used by the Elmdon villagers to talk about their ideas of localism and class.

achievement can be rewarded through *self*-mobility — that is, a person may better his/her own class position." (Ibid.:51)[26] This modelling of class relations sets up an inherent antithesis between fixed strata and mobile individuals; persons are at one and the same time seen as defined by, and having the potential for altering, their class position. The "... English construction of individuality as constituting a natural resistance to social units ... [puts] ... the idea of the individual in a particular relationship to the social units he or she is placed in, such that movement between units is theoretically possible." (Ibid.) Strathern assumed that these issues are highly relevant for understanding the implications of localism. The local community as a bounded natural unit, whose boundary can nevertheless be crossed, replicates the idea of permeable class boundaries (Ibid.:51-52).

Strathern's ideas are not only relevant for the understanding of English society, they may also inspire further interesting insights into the modelling of class relations and the relations of local culture and class elsewhere in Britain. For the upper, and to some extend the upper middle class, in Scotland and Wales, an Anglicized background (English education, "English" values, etc.) is still essential for their identity (cf. Emmett 1964, Khleif 1980, Nadel-Klein 1991). Strathern's concept may help us understand the seemingly paradoxical relationship of the idea of rootedness and localism, and the emphasis on the ability or necessity of transcending localism, which is important for the identity of the local elite in North Angus described by Nadel-Klein. "The assertion that localism is opposed to their own self-image is an intimate part of elite culture. In this upper-class 'folk model,' travel enables one to 'broaden'; it also entitles one to dominate." (Nadel-Klein 1991:513) However, if we examine Nadel-Klein's description of the local landowning elite more closely, the rejection of localism by the upper class is revealed as being rather ambiguous. The claim of being entitled to dominate derives its power not only from the ability to transcend the local community, but also from the very rootedness within the locality. Nadel-Klein (1991:510-511) described the case of "Edward", who, she stated, exemplified the group of the old landowning elite of North Angus:

"He explained his active local service to me in terms of tradition: 'Our family has been here such a long time, we really have an immense obligation to do something for the community. This house has founda-

---

26 Strathern argued that class as such is conceptualized analogous to labour as a natural possession belonging to a person. That labour capacity can be appropriated by another to whom it then belongs, is a crucial, and at the same time "... rather bizarre, element in this model of personhood. " (Strathern 1984:51)

tions that go back to the time of King Edward I. And I'm the laird.' When I asked him what it meant to be 'the laird,' he said it was part of the tradition of hereditary landownership:

My father was called the laird of Craig, and the children in Ferryden and on the farms roundabout still call me 'the lairdie,' even though the estate is smaller now. I have an excellent relationship with the villagers, quite warm and affectionate. Some of them still tip their hats when I go down to the post office. Really, I suppose it means leadership. It's still delightfully feudal around here, you know, and the villagers are so sweet."

Furthermore, within the communities of the *Celtic Fringe*, the "Welsh" and "Scottish" concepts of class relations, and the predominantly "English" concept of class relations, are apparently competing with each other. Welsh and Scottish concepts of class relations are, of course, informed by the realities of economic centre-periphery relations — which produced a feeling of being exploited or deliberately underdeveloped by the English upper class — but they are also informed by different cultural concepts of status. The question of the character of class relations, and the changing importance of class and status as categories in interpersonal relations is, I believe, one of the most important issues the social anthropology of rural communities has to face.

Peter G. Mewett (1982b:124-125), for example, found that class differences in Clachan on the Isle of Lewis — at the time of his fieldwork during the 1970s — had not yet been translated into interpersonal differentiation. Nevertheless, he argued that changes in the concept of class were inevitable because one of the barriers to the emergence of class distinctions — intimate knowledge of members and the "way of life" of the community which makes meanings sharable — will become less significant due to the increasing individuation in social relations: "My view is that the combination of an increase in economic differentiation and in the projection of prestige markers, together with a decrease in the multiplexity of social relations, will culminate in the emergence of class as a means of classifying interpersonal relations." That social change is a central theme of community studies in Britain, is also evident in Mewett's (1988) analysis of the context of out-migration from Lewis. Mewett showed quite clearly how the wider British society has influenced the indigenous perception of life on the island. Migration has been an economic necessity for the islanders since the nineteenth century. Today, however, mere survival is no longer the only incentive for emigration. In fact, the island could support a much larger population "... if people were willing to live on unemployment benefits." (Mewett 1988:211) Mewett argued, that the reasons for the emigration of a large percentage of the population, suggested that ideas about standard of living were an integral part of the islander's economic reasoning. The conclusion drawn by most islanders, that Lewis cannot offer an adequate standard of living, is the result of an implicit comparison with the wider British society "... which provides the source of the ideas about that which constitutes acceptable material standards. From all angles the island loses out. Island issues do not set the parameters of current perception of economic life but, when evaluated against these, Lewis is seen as being woefully inadequate. ... Despite the emotive attachment retained with island-based social relationships, the negative evaluation of island life means that Lewis people face the stigma of failure unless they either work or train away from the island. By moving 'away', the person proves a personal ability to cope with the conditions set by the wider society, something that cannot be done at 'home'. Migration, therefore, has become a normative aspect of social life in Lewis." (Ibid.:212) Although rural communities are negatively evaluated where economic opportunities are concerned, those who leave the community for economic reasons nevertheless retain a deep emotional attachment to it. "This tension between two opposed valuations of the small community is, of course, generalised throughout the British Isles in the sustained increase of urban as opposed to rural population, and the emptying of remote areas, which has as its converse the migration of the urban middle class to the part-time alternative society of the weekend cottage." (Chapman 1978:204) Return migrants and "urban refugees" (to borrow a term from Diana Forsythe (1980:287)) create an increasingly complex network of relationships between rural and urban cultures and can cause some major changes and conflicts in rural communities.

All these studies show that British social anthropology has produced valuable insights into different perceptions of the British class system. They have improved our understanding of the complex relationships between local cultures and the wider British society. However, Nadel-Klein's criticism (see page 59) of Cohen's approach as being too preoccupied with the view from the inside is still relevant. Apparently, most anthropological studies of communities have remained tied to the local context or have not placed enough emphasis on the relations between community and the wider society.

Yet, the "new wave" of anthropology at home has not only contributed to our understanding of different cultures in the British Isles it has also stimulated the debate — essentially a debate between the so-called postmodernist anthropologists — about reflexivity. Modern social anthropology developed essentially as the study of people and cultures that were far removed from the cultural context which had produced anthropology. The problem, however, was not — what many sociologists seemed to believe (see pages 32-33 for Bell and Newby's critique) — that the anthropological techniques designed for the study of "other" cultures were not adequate for studying advanced industrial societies, rather it was a problem of the anthropologist's perception and conceptualization of both "the other" and "home" in relation to the production of "knowledge".

At the 1985 ASA Conference on *Anthropology at Home*, Marilyn Strathern has warned us that the idea of peripherality of rural communities may be effectively blocking "... our understanding of the way their self-acknowledged differences draw on common British ideas *about* difference." (Strathern 1987:17, footnote 1) For all of us, "home" implies a certain degree of familiarity, however, the problem that familiarity, the feeling of being at home, poses, is evident in Audrey Richards' vivid description of the advantages and disadvantages of being a resident and an observer in the community she studied. In contrast to her experiences in African communities, the situation as an English woman in an English village was totally different. In the African communities she had studied, she was accepted as a learner and the differences in language, education, clothing, life style and skin colour were too great for her to become identified with the local inhabitants. In Elmdon, however, there "... was no need to explain my presence. I was just an outsider — 'a lady from Cambridge' — who was a familiar sight, since I had lived in the village for five years before the survey began. Nor was there any necessity to explain Elmdon ways of living to me although I, in common with most of the students, had not lived in an English village before and had much to learn about patterns of Essex agriculture and housekeeping." (Richards 1981:xviii) Strathern (1987:16) has shown, that the grounds of familiarity and distance are shifting ones and that it is necessary to rescue "... the concept of home from impossible measurements of degrees of familiarity." It is exactly this continuum of familiarity which obscures the conceptual break between the anthropologist's concepts and those the investigated themselves produce. Therefore, Strathern argued (1987:16-17) that, one must also know "... whether or not investigator/investigated are equally at home, as it were, with the kinds of premises about social life which inform anthropological enquiry. One suspects that while Travellers and Malay villagers are not so at home, in their talk about 'community', 'socialization', or 'class', for example, Elmdoners are." The question whether or not the anthropologist is at home can only be answered by looking at the end-product of his labour: the text. The criterion for such a distinction is the cultural continuity of the anthropologist's product with the account produced by the people who were studied. It is because the construct of the "other" is constituted by our knowledge about ourselves, that the goal of what Strathern (1987) has called "auto-anthropology" is an enhanced critical awareness of ourselves. This does not imply, that an increasing reflexivity is only a means for the anthropologist to improve his self-consciousness, for "... a conceptual reflexivity exists outside the sensitivities of individual practitioners ...". An important criterion is the extent to which the outcome of the "... anthropological processing of 'knowledge' draws on concepts which also belong to the society and culture under study ..."; in other words, the extent to which the anthropological text, does or does not render people's conceptions back to themselves (Strathern 1987:18).

Yet, the study of Elmdon showed that, what had started as continuity — villagers and anthropologists held nearly the same world view — ended in disjunction. This disjunction resulted from the fact that firstly, ethnographic texts are hardly continuous with indigenous narrative from — the account was not rendered back in the form it had been given — , and secondly, that indigenous reflections are incorporated as data and cannot be taken as the framing of the data. The inevitable conclusion is, "... that there is always a discontinuity between the indigenous understanding and the analytic concepts which frame ethnography itself. These derive from a specific theoretical focus which may make intelligible the anthropologist's behaviour (as an 'academic') but not necessarily what he/she writes." (Ibid.) Central to the dilemma of form (anthropological and/or indigenous) is the manner in which ethnographic authority is constructed in reference to the informants, and the part they are given in the anthropological texts — the informant is not recognizable as an author. However, it would not be sufficient to restore the subjectivity of the indigenous author by a "... construction preserving dialogue and producing discourse rather than text ..." (Strathern 1987:19). The critical question is the productive activity that lies behind the informant's verbal expression and his/her relationship to its contents. "Without knowing how they 'own' their words, we cannot know what we have done in appropriating them." (Ibid.) Thus, the form in which the anthropologist's productive activity becomes the basis for the relationship between himself/herself and the selves under study is the critical factor. During the process of anthropological analysis, the actors' meanings may be replaced, more or less, by a meaning constructed by the anthropologist. The crucial question is, whether the anthropological framing remains an external "explanation", or whether the indigenous type of explanation will be replaced by the anthropological type. In case of replacement the anthropologist will have substituted his/her authorship of events for those who gave them meaning in the first place. Strathern suggested (Strathern 1987:25) that "... this might be a significant element in any irritation expressed by Elmdon villagers: that my version of events supplanted theirs—in not reproducing their descriptions in their own genre I had, as it were, displaced their authorship of the narrative. It is important to note, of course, that this displacement could not occur if the ensuing account were not in some way regarded as a version of their own accounts (e.g. that both 'explained' something)."

In order to analyze the process of authoring, Strathern distinguished between the anthropologist as an *author* and as a *writer*. In relation to the people studied outside his/her own cultural context the anthropologist is a *writer*. As a *writer*, he/she is not replacing authorship because he/she is not producing a new version for the people concerned. "*Writing* is used as a vehicle for explanation via comparison, above all the comparison of ideas from different social sources whose origins can be juxtaposed." (Ibid., emphasis added) However, for the readership at home the anthropologist is an author — he/she is in total control of the access to the "other" his/her readership will have. The fundamental contradiction that ethnographic research produces — between personal and prolonged interaction with the "other" and construction of the "other" in terms of distance — is negotiated through the separation of the roles of *author* and *writer*. The first allows the experience in the field to validate authorship for the home readership. "The second allows a theoretically constructed distance (fabricated at home) to inform the job of writer *vis-à-vis* the narratives and texts provided by the informants (in the field)." (Ibid.) In respect to anthropology at home, the distinction between *author* and *writer* is still valid but of a different structure. Strathern (1987:26) argued that the ethnographer at home becomes an author in relationship to those being studied because there is a cultural continuity between his/her cultural constructs and theirs — there is a general agreement that culture or society can be objects of study, furthermore, terms like "relationships", "roles", "community" are used by both, the anthropologist and the people being studied[27]. However, the anthropologist seems to be using these ideas in different ways. The anthropological analysis may thus appear to give a further view which encompasses and overrides the original explanations and thereby supplants them. These new versions can, of course, always be challenged[28]. " The possibility of authors supplanting one another comes from conceptual-izations of productive activity as a process by which useful things are made out of materials thereby relativized as useless. People may object to the value put on what they supply." (Ibid.) To his/her main readership, his/her colleagues, the ethnographer at home remains a writer. If we assume that anthropologists at home will achieve a greater understanding, then the anthropologist as an author, who illuminates people's experiences in a different way, may contribute to an increasing self-knowledge of the people themselves[29]. Further, the anthropologist as a writer also offers a reflection on the basis of analysis to his/her colleagues. "Knowing ourselves better both as objects of study and as the subjects doing the study:

---

27 The question is, whether or not, this supposed "cultural continuity" is really continuous. I believe that by presupposing cultural continuity the fallacious idea of a culturally homogeneous United Kingdom may return through the back-door.

28 An interesting description of the reactions of the Whalsay Islanders to his articles on their community (see Cohen 1982c, 1982d) was published by Cohen. He wrote: "These were read by many people on the island. Although little was said to me direct, I sensed somewhat mixed feelings. Our own friends seemed quite untroubled by anything I had written; other people professed themselves 'amused' or 'interested'. There were rumours of some muted concern among one group from one or two other people whom I knew hardly at all. One night in 1984 a young man to whom I had previously rarely spoken and who was not connected with anyone about whom I had written, questioned me pointedly (most un-Whalsa'-like behaviour) in the club about my own kinship and ethnic origins." (Cohen 1987:206)

29 This is a point which Dell Hymes had argued almost twenty years earlier. In 1969, he said that the ethnographer mediated between the specific knowledge of those he studied and the general knowledge "... usually entirely in the direction of the latter, as represented in a professional community and publication. As far as possible, the mediation must go also the other way—even primarily the other way." (Hymes 1974:54)

the two are fused in the cultural premise that all knowledge is a species of self-knowledge." (Strathern 1987:27) In case of anthropology, such self-knowledge can only be expressed as a dialectical process: "... the auto-anthropologist comes from a culture/society that 'has' a concept of culture/ society. Whether anthropologists are at home *qua* anthropologists, is not to be decided by whether they call themselves Malay, belong to the Travellers or have been born in Essex; it is decided by the relationship between their techniques of organizing knowledge and how people organize knowledge themselves." (Strathern 1987:31)

Ardener and Strathern have called attention to the fact that the imposition of our definitions of other people's identity, in terms of "... comfortingly drifting layers of binary oppositions: development/ underdevelopment, traditional/modern, centre/periphery ...", may lead to symbolic expropriation of the people's identity (Ardener 1987:43-44). Edwin Ardener (1987) contributed an interesting perspective to this problem in relation to the ideas of *remoteness* and *remote areas*. The basic paradox of remote areas, which Ardener assumed to be "a law of 'remote' areas", is that the feeling of remoteness persists even when the "remote" area has been reached — when it is present. Apparently, remoteness does not protect the remote areas, because the people from cultures outside theses areas, those who define them as being remote, have an ambivalent feeling of love-hate for them. Remote areas seem to be subject to alternating periods of idealization and denigration, such that Ardener asked: "After the destruction of one generation of strangers how is it that they are asked to play the role of ideal society to the next, before being unthinkingly redeveloped or underdeveloped out of existence by the next?" (Ardener 1987:43) This paradox stems from the conceptualization of their identity which ignores the experienced reality of a person's identity. The social space, however, consists of persons who, regardless of other people's perceptions and constructions, experience themselves as real. The inhabitants of remote areas, like the Hebrides, see themselves as ordinary people not in the least resembling the artistic or textual remoteness imposed upon them by the outside world. "They are quite ordinary – as ordinary as anybody can be who has the regular experience of wild-eyed romantics tottering through his door." (Ardener 1987:45) Ardener argued that to answer the question of what life in a remote area will mean for the identity of its inhabitants we must consider some interesting paradoxes.

These paradoxes arise from the double-perception of remote areas (see Ardener 1987:45-48).

Ardener suggested (1987:48) that the paradox of remote areas can be seen as systematic. He (1987:49-50) considered remote areas to be "event-rich" or "event-dense" — in contrast to the "large stable systems of dominant central area" which are "event-poor". He argued that events are defined within social space by a certain quality that he called "significance". However, many things that happen have only an "automaton-like quality" for the participants, which means that they are not considered to be an event. "Essentially, specifying something in the space introduces a singularity into it, which 'twists off' the specified. The latter is bounded one way – from the perspective of the specifier." In the central areas there are more automatisms and fewer major singularities occur. Remote areas as a part of a wider definitional space, the dominant state, will perceive themselves as a singularity in that space[30]. Furthermore, all individuals are potential singularities in social space, and since remote areas are singularities in a wider social space the singularities (individuals) within are reinforced. Singularity is perceived differently from the outside than from the inside. Therefore, remote areas are marked by a double specification: from the outside they are perceived and specified as being remote, from the inside people have their own different perception which is "... a counter-specification of the dominant, or defining space, working in the opposite direction." The double specification, experienced as intrusion and vulnerability by those inside the remote area, also leads to an overdefinition or overdetermination of individuality. In the case of remote areas event-richness means that in the face of the continuous threat to the maintenance of the self-generated social definitions, the defining power of the individuals is enhanced and singularities are continuously generated. This process makes the "disenchainment" of individuals and the overdetermination of individuality possible. However, the condition of remoteness is not related to the periphery but to the dominant defining "centre" — certain, but not all, geographical peripheries are not properly linked to the centre. Ardener argued "... that while human beings have theoretically unlimited classifying power, not all classifications have equal experiential density." Remote areas are of great theoretical interest because the people who are defined as 'remote' are intermittently conscious of the defining processes of others

---

30 Event-richness can not only occur within remote areas but also in any social space.

that might absorb them. "That is why they are the very crucibles of the creation of identity, why they are of the great theoretical interest, and why social anthropologists 'at home' may be very far away indeed."

Since the early days of community studies it has been evident that the study of communities in a modern industrialized environment is necessarily a study of change. With the advent of the community studies revival, the evolutionary explanations of change, that were so fashionable until the 1960s, had to make way for a different way of thinking. The anthropology of rural communities à la Anthony P. Cohen is more a study of the effects than of the process of change. The focus lies on the experience of change by the individual and the collectivity to which he/she belongs. What the otherwise totally different approaches of the nineteenth century and the community studies revival have in common is an implicit or explicit critique of modern industrial society. Although the critique is now couched in terms of the discourse of identity, which is more immediate to the experience of change than the rather abstract evolutionary assumptions of Durkheim and Tönnies, there is still an element of academic romanticism to be found in the description of community. Many sociologists will certainly argue that this romanticism is due to the refusal of social anthropologists to approach the subject scientifically. However, the development of the subject has shown that the anthropologists effort to distance himself/herself from the people and culture he/she studied by trying to become a scientist was especially problematic — and perhaps even schizophrenic — in the case of anthropology at home. Analogous to Strathern's assumption that the anthropologist replaces the meanings of his informants with his own (see pages 69-70), one could also argue, that during the process of producing *science* the anthropologist, in a way, replaces his/her own meaning and authorship by a meaning extraneous to himself/herself — *scientific* version supplants his/her *version*. The danger is inherent in the common assumption that science represents "objective meaning", "truth". This view of science is likely to be shared by the anthropologists and the people he/she studies and is, therefore, likely to inform their evaluation of the anthropologist's account. The anthropologist's *version* — the ethnographer-centred ethnographic fiction — can be freely challenged, however, the anthropologist's displaced scientific version, now regarded as "objective truth", can definitely be regarded as a replacement of the subjective meaning of his informants which is far more difficult to challenge. Therefore, anthropology at home, like anthropology elsewhere, has to be critically aware of its own process of "knowledge-production". Anthropology at home — the anthropology of a culture/society that produced the concept of culture/society — can perhaps be more immediate to an anthropology of anthropology than anthropology elsewhere, because the anthropologist is less able to remain a writer in relation to those he studied (provided that he/she does not loose the cross-cultural perspective). When anthropological knowledge is more directly challengeable, the anthropologist will be more immediately held responsible for the picture of the other he has painted — this may heighten the anthropologist's critical awareness of the consequence his account may have for the people he studied. Critical introspection is the order of the day. In this sense, anthropology at home has provided interesting and far-reaching insights into the indigenous cultures of the British Isles including anthropology itself. However, there is still a lot of work, and critical reflection, to be done, especially in respect to the rather unsatisfactory situation of ethnographic research in Wales. This will be evident in the next chapter when we will look at the short "era" of ethnographic research in Wales in the 1950s.

7 THE DRAGON HAS MANY FACES

ECONOMY AND SOCIETY IN WALES

In regard to Wales, the community studies revival in social anthropology has passed by virtually unnoticed. The fact that the study of rural communities in Wales has apparently vanished from research agenda of social anthropology in Britain is quite surprising since such studies were initiated by Alwyn D. Rees and his students at the University College of Wales at Aberystwyth (see Rees 1950; Davies & Rees 1960). The political developments of the 1970s — mainly the rise of *Plaid Cymru*, the nationalist Party of Wales, and the devolution debate and the following disaster of the devolution referendum in 1979 (see also pages 87-88) — have not stimulated a return to qualitative anthropological field research methods in the study of Welsh communities. For sociology, on the other hand, these developments provided an "initial kick" for a new sociology of Wales and put an end to, what Glyn Williams (1986:176) has described as, "disciplinary ethnocentrism" — sociology at Welsh universities was until the 1970s almost exclusively oriented towards England. Day (1986:153) stated, that confidence was restored to sociologists working in the periphery "… that their contribution to social science need not automatically be relegated to the category of the quaint and parochial." As we have seen in chapter four, the view of the United Kingdom as a homogeneous society was thoroughly revised during the 1970s, and consequently, the study of peripheral cultures in Britain was invested with new importance. Following the general trend in sociology (see pages 28-30), however, community studies were temporarily abandoned by Welsh sociologists in the 1970s. Sociology was much more concerned with macro-level processes; the perspectives which dominated Welsh sociology since the mid 1970s were derived from current trends in the sociology of development.

Michael Hechter's (1975) "Internal Colonialism" was the first contribution to the sociology of Wales that was inspired by the sociology of development (see pages 56-57). He was concerned with the persistence of separate ethnic identity in the Celtic Fringe of the British Isles and tried to explain the relative failure of national development in the United Kingdom (Hechter 1975:11). To achieve his analytical goals he employed the model of *internal colonialism*, which places Wales and Scotland (conceived as the *periphery*: the Celtic *Fringe*) in the wider British context as a dependent internal colony of the English *core*. Hechter assumed that there are several culturally distinct and regionally concentrated groups: the dominant culture of the core extending from the political centre, and the subordinate cultures of the periphery. The relationship between the core and periphery is characterized by political incorporation, economic dependence, and cultural exclusion of the periphery. As a result of the political incorporation of the Celtic regions by the English state the development in these regions was based on exogenous, rather than endogenous forces. The economy of these internal colonies was forced into a development which was complementary to the development of the dominant English society. External control of economic development by members of the dominant society put severe constrains on the development of industry in the dominated areas. The industry was highly specialized in the production of raw materials and a narrow range of primary commodities, and was, as a result, forced into dependency on external markets. Central to Hechter's model is the assumption that the colonial development produced a cultural division of labour. This is evident in the stratification system which is based upon ethnic/cultural differences that cut across class categories. The key positions are reserved to members of the dominant culture, while the indigenous population is confined to subordinate positions. Hechter argued that the distinction between the core and periphery in terms of social solidarity is very similar to Weber's distinction between class and status group. Membership of a class does not necessarily imply class solidarity because class assumes individual orientation to the market, whereas, the membership of a status group implies collective orientation, and therefore solidarity. Class and status are presented as alternative systems of stratification. The cultural division of labour confines the members of the peripheral culture to low class positions in the dominant stratification system of the core. However, through maintaining their cultural institutions and identity they will be able to define their position within a different stratification system based on status. Thus, the salience of ethnic identity in the Celtic Fringe is due to the increasing inequalities between core and periphery which create a cultural division of labour. (Hechter 1975)

Hechter's model was taken up with some enthusiasm by the Welsh intelligentsia because it gave "scientific" backing for the lamented cultural oppression of the Welsh by the English (Day 1986:169, see also Hechter 1985:19-20), but it has also been much criticized by social scientists "... for lumping together disparate regions and periods of history, for misreading economics, for economic reductionism, for confusing unofficial practices with official state policies, and for misuse and misunderstanding of the term 'colonialism' ... . His model has great difficulty in accommodating the changes in peripheral cultures (for example the decline of regional languages) as Hechter himself recognises." (Grillo 1989:82)

In his critique of Hechter's model, Nairn (1981:201) accused Hechter of "... the fundamental error of locating Scotland in the 'Celtic Fringe' at all." Nairn (1981) argued, that Scotland had recently entered a state of being "relatively overdeveloped" in relation to the larger British state which dominates it politically. Previously, Scotland was an old industrial society with its native capitalist class, which developed at approximately the same rate as the larger state it was linked to. However, as a result of the dramatic decline of industrial England and the "... sudden differential impetus given to the Scottish middle class by North Sea oil production ..." a crisis of uneven development arose. "Ever more clearly, the outlook of the previously rather quiescent Scottish bourgeoisie is one of restive impatience with English 'backwardness', London muddle, economic incompetence, state parasitism, and so forth." (Nairn 1981:204) In a later article on internal colonialism, Hechter (1985) admitted that Nairn had been correct in arguing that Scotland is a relatively overdeveloped peripheral region. He now argued that the fact that the Scottish people have been energetic and successful innovators in the British context did not correspond to the image of a typical colony. However, he did not correct his interpretation of Wales as an internal colony, probably because his book was so well received by Welsh nationalists. He proudly declared that the "... book was quickly adopted into the platform of the Welsh Nationalist Party (Plaid Cymru) ...", and that sales of the book were booming in the Welsh universities (Hechter 1985:20).

In relation to Scotland and the wider European context the development of Wales is quite peculiar and, therefore, Nairn has placed it in between, what he called, underdeveloped and overdeveloped countries.

On the one hand, Wales shared many features of forced under-development like, depopulation of rural areas, cultural oppression, fragmentary development, etc. . On the other hand, Wales was also a centre of the industrial revolution in the nineteenth century. However, while the South was industrialized the central, northern and western parts of Wales remained rural, agricultural areas — with few exceptions, one being the slate mining areas in Gwynedd. Merfyn Jones (1980:203-204) has argued that Gwynedd was in fact a core area of early capitalist development and that it was not as remote as has often been assumed. The rapid development of the slate and copper industries confirmed that the area was indeed a centre of early capitalist development. Especially in North Wales and Mid-Wales, several of the pre-capitalist institutions were retained because capitalist expansion took the line of least resistance and was a matter of transforming the scale of production, rather than increasing the productivity through technological innovation (Lovering 1983:52-53). Thus, a pattern of economic specialization developed, within which the new industries were enclaves in an otherwise marginally changed economic environment. In contrast to Scotland, the development of an autonomous Welsh industrial bourgeoisie was inhibited. Wales, which prior to the industrial revolution had almost no native bourgeoisie and only a small and thoroughly Anglicized indigenous aristocracy, acquired an English or highly Anglicized bourgeoisie.

Parallel to the growth of industry there was an equal growth of religious nonconformity in the late nineteenth century promoted by Methodists, Baptists, and other denominations. The numbers of Nonconformists in Wales had increased rapidly since the mid-eighteenth century and religion played the dominant part in the social life of Welsh communities. The majority of the Welsh people became members of Nonconformist chapels (cf. Morgan 1982:14) which promoted all kinds of Welsh cultural activities — Welsh was used as the language of worship, they also organized *eisteddfodau*[31], and provided educational facilities in the Sunday Schools. In contrast to the Nonconformist chapels, the English state church (the Anglican Church in Wales), which was patronized by the Anglicized gentry,

---

31 Plural of *eisteddfod*: Welsh festival with literary and musical contests. *Eisteddfodau* are held exclusively in the Welsh language — with the exception of the International Eisteddfod held annually in Llangollen which is an international folk festival. They have an important function as symbolic markers of distinctiveness to the outside world, and as rituals confirming the unity of the Welsh community.

was only supported by a small minority of the population. Morgan (1982:90) argued that religious nonconformity gave a further impetus to popular involvement in Welsh cultural and religious experience which had been developed basically in the new towns in Wales. The migration of Welsh-speaking people to the new towns gave a new urban and institutional direction to Welsh culture. In these towns Welsh national consciousness flourished. The encompassing Welsh cultural identity was not fostered by a broad-based bourgeoisie, rather, it was created by the Nonconformist Welsh elite, which David Smith (1980:218) has called the "clerisy". The "clerisy"—preachers, teachers, printers, shopkeepers, and lawyers—were "... the almost incidental by-product of the Welsh educational tradition and of nineteenth century growth, briefly refulgent with the hopeful confluence of the two." (Smith 1980:219) Charlotte Aull Davies (1983:203) assumed that the "democratic" structure of the Nonconformist chapels encouraged the development of a local social structure with an elite which was relatively divorced from the structure in which the English-oriented aristocracy and bourgeoisie were located—an assumption which certainly resonates with Hechter's idea of the reaction of the indigenous elite to the cultural division of labour. The concept of Welsh national identity was developed into a cultural-linguistic nationalism by the cultural movement of the late nineteenth century. Welsh nationalism "... created something like the cultural form, the tracery of a nation where no state had existed. It became a substantial force in the new civil society of 19th and 20th century Wales, even without political, legal, and other institutions." (Nairn 1981:210) The Welsh middle class of the late nineteenth century saw itself as standing at the forefront of the modernization of Wales. Its strong Nonconformist values became an instrument for creating a non-class ideology; an ideology which covered the often contradictory, and potentially destructive, interests and passions in Wales (Gwyn A. Williams 1991:234). The concept of the *gwerin* represents such a non-class ideology. The term *gwerin* denotes a people undivided by class categories — the upper class is only included in the concept as a negative boundary marker — and a community in a social and geographical sense. The *gwerin* was a construct which was imbued with meaning through the reproduction of "traditional" Welsh habits and the acceptance of a moral order outlined by Nonconformist values. It was a Welsh-speaking, educated, egalitarian and respectable, but on the whole genially poor or small propertied people. "This *gwerin* was the heart and soul of the Welsh nation who cultivated a respectable and genial commonality, free from the 'side' and the 'snobbishness' so characteristic of the English. It was warm, mutually supportive, often cosy and rather amateur sort of fellowship within a hard, pushy, beady-eyed general society dominated by the English and their language, philistine and commercial." (Gwyn A. Williams 1991:237-238) Williams argued that the term *gwerin* is virtually untranslatable into English and is perhaps similar to the "Spanish" concept of the *pueblo*. However, it is not clear to which concept of *pueblo* Williams refers. In his study of the Andalusian community of Alcalá, Julian Pitt-Rivers (1954) distinguished between three meanings of *pueblo*: (1) the expression of a human community in geographical terms, (2) the feeling of belonging to the community, and (3) people in the sense of common people as opposed to the rich. For the people of Alcalá the third meaning of *pueblo* is "... synonymous with the other meanings, for the rich do not really belong to the pueblo but to that wider world which has already been delimited as theirs." (Pitt-Rivers 1954:18) In her study of the Basque community of Elgeta, Marianne Heiberg (1989:142-149), has defined the *pueblo* as a "moral community" which corresponds more closely to the concept of the *gwerin*. The term *pueblo* is a moral notion which is related to the self-image of the villagers. The moral values and the behavioural prescriptions they generated covered most aspects of village life. The *pueblo* was regarded as egalitarian, respectable, hard-working, demanding total commitment to the interests of the community, and as Basque. When religion, which had provided a fundamental aspect of community values, declined, nationalist sentiment and ethnicity provided important moral values. The *pueblo* consisted of two concentric circles, the inner core of those who complied to the moral norms of the pueblo and those who fulfilled some of the important criteria for inclusion but not all, like industrialists, who were morally suspect because of their economic position. However, the village professionals like doctors, teachers, etc. were, in contrast to Wales, all outsiders and not included in the *pueblo*. As in case of the indigenous industrialists in Elgeta, the Welsh "service bourgeoisie" (Gwyn A. Williams 1991:238) was sufficiently close to their *gwerin* roots to preserve the one-class ideology, despite the apparent contradictions the very existence of a bourgeoisie created. In Wales, the emphasis on language has served as a means to mask the widening gap between the *gwerin* and later the *working class* ideal and the reality of growing class differences inside the rural communities.

Even though the South was industrially developed, this development, as Day (1986) quite rightly concluded, was essentially one-sided. The role of Wales as a supplier of raw materials, basic products and labour, resulted in a rapid succession of industries. These industries were at first extensively exploited, the profits were transferred to England, and afterwards, in the face of falling profits, rapidly abandoned. Until the 1920s the economy of Wales was sufficiently dynamic to prevent total impoverishment and mass emigration. However, with the decline of the world and British economies during the 1920s the Welsh economy — which was totally dependent on the wider economy and forced to produce primarily for Britain's export trade — collapsed. Now, the price for over-specialization had to be paid, and the price was high. Unemployment reached 38%[32] and in the period between 1921 and 1939 almost 500,000 people were forced to emigrate. The rural areas suffered from depopulation and the industrial areas from long-term unemployment. At the end of the 1930s Wales seemed to be on the road to prolonged impoverishment (Day 1986:163-164). In South Wales the devastating effects of the economic collapse led to "... depression and despair which crushed its society for almost twenty years and left ineradicable scars upon its consciousness." (Morgan 1982:210)

In the rural areas of Wales the situation was not much better because agriculture stagnated. Although, policy changes had weakened the control of the old landowning class over the state which led to a considerable change in the pattern of landownership, most of the new owners were heavily burdened with mortgages and did not posses enough capital to modernize the machinery. The proportion of agricultural holdings occupied by the owner increased form 10.6% in 1909 to 37% in 1941 (Glyn Williams 1980:170-171). The rural areas suffered from a continuously increasing depopulation which had negative effects on the reproduction and the maintenance of Welsh cultural distinctiveness (Morgan 1982:220). As a result of massive immigration from England to the industrial areas of South Wales at the turn of the century, and emigration from the Welsh-speaking rural and industrial areas after the collapse of the Welsh economy, the number of Welsh-speakers decreased from 43.5% in 1911 to 37.2% in

---

32 During the inter-war period unemployment rates in the industrialized valleys of South Wales were exceptionally high. In 1935 unemployment stood at over 51% in the Merthyr Vale, and at over 40% in the Rhondda and Aberdare valleys (Morgan 1981:215).

33 Morgan's figures differ slightly from those given by Colin Williams (see Fig. 3).

	1921	1931	1951	1961	1971	1981
Wales	**37.1**	**36.8**	**28.9**	**26.0**	**20.8**	**18.9**
Counties						
Clwyd	41.7	41.3	30.2	27.3	21.4	18.7
Dyfed	67.8	69.1	63.3	60.1	52.5	46.3
Gwent	5.0	4.7	2.8	2.9	1.9	2.5
Gwynedd	78.7	82.5	74.2	71.4	64.7	61.2
Powys	35.1	34.6	29.6	27.8	23.7	20.2
South Glamorgan	6.3	6.1	4.7	5.2	5.0	5.8
Mid-Glamorgan	38.4	37.1	22.8	18.5	10.5	8.4
West Glamorgan	41.3	40.5	31.6	27.5	20.3	16.4

(cf. Colin H. Williams 1984:116, table 1)

Fig. 3 Proportion of Welsh-speakers by county (1921-1981)

1931 (Morgan 1982:243)[33]. Furthermore, the census data showed that the country was linguistically divided and that the decline of the Welsh language was dramatic — the majority of the population in South Wales was English-speaking, while in the northern and western parts of Wales the majority of the population was Welsh-speaking. Not only the Welsh language, but Welsh society and identity as a whole, experienced a deep crisis. Kenneth O. Morgan (1982:239) wrote: "The onset of economic depression brought obvious and visible strains to the fabric of Welsh society and culture. More insidious and less apparent, but equally worrying for a growing number of contemporaries, was the emergence of more formidable cultural barriers than had hitherto existed between those who did and those who did not speak the Welsh language. The changing balance between these two communities added to the tension of life in the inter-war period." A reaction to the decline of Welsh economy and language during the 1920s was the foundation of *Plaid Genedlaethol Cymru* (the National Party of Wales, later *Plaid Cymru*) during the Pwllheli Eisteddfod in 1925. The party was founded by middle class intellectuals and was advocating a conservative and romantic nationalism based on the "values" of Welsh culture and Christianity. Saunders Lewis — whom Kenneth O. Morgan

(1982:247) has characterized as the "... exponent of the anti-democratic Catholic ethos ..."³⁴ — provided Welsh nationalism with its philosophical foundations. He constructed an ideology that was based on the assumption that the recovery of Welsh identity could only be achieved by a return to the values of medieval Welsh society, because the Middle Ages were a time when Welsh civilization was still unpoluted by pagan materialism (cf. Grillo 1989:93; Morgan 1982:206-208; Osmond 1978:173-175, 239-240). The romantic idea of *Gemeinschaft* was central to Plaid Cymru's ideology. The Welsh community was conceptualized as the natural unit, the organic whole, the archetype of *Gemeinschaft*, which was crucial for the development and maintenance of identity. Moreover, the Welsh community and with it the language — perceived as the very heart of Welshness³⁵ — was believed to be threatened by the alienating effects of English and capitalist rule. The close connection of language and identity deepened the rift between Welsh-speaking and English-speaking Welshmen. By denying that a person who did not speak Welsh could have a Welsh identity, the identity of the majority of the Welsh people — those who were monoglot English-speakers — was simply negated. Even though the English-speaking Welsh were denied the status of true Welshmen, they were trying to come to terms with their *Welsh* identity. They were in a difficult position in between the English and the Welsh, stigmatized as Welshmen by the English, and not accepted as Welshmen by the Welsh-speaking "true" Welshmen. As a result of the growing polarization of Welsh society the concept of "Anglo-Welsh" culture began to arise during the 1930s. "The fact increasingly dawned that an inability to speak Welsh did not mean that a man or woman had lost his or her sense of Welsh nationality, or an involvement with the cultural and national problems." (Morgan 1982:258) Morgan argued that the cultural divide became more pronounced during the Second World War because the pressure on the rural Welsh communities increased, the decline of the Welsh language continued, and English culture — in the form of evacuees from England and English soldiers — poured into Wales through all kinds of channels (Morgan 1982:269-70). Nevertheless, the war also stimulated

---

34 Saunders Lewis was a Catholic which was quite unusual in the predominantly Nonconformist Welsh nationalist circles.

35 A well known nationalist slogan—"A nation without a language, is a nation without a heart!"—is frequently used in Wales to illustrate the fact that the language is perceived as the core of Welsh identity.

a strategic decentralization of industry, and the first substantial manufacturing employment was brought to Wales (Day 1986:165).

After the war, the state tried to overcome the problem of regional imbalances by direct intervention in the form of nationalization of industries, subsidization and directive planning. Even though these policies caused a rise in manufacturing employment from 17% in 1921 to 29% in 1971, the structure of the Welsh economy was still not diversified enough to secure autonomous development. Furthermore, Wales had to compete with other marginal areas who could also offer subsidies, cheap capital, and cheap and poorly organized labour. Economic development in Wales continued in a dependent mode, which meant that the capital was not really committed to the development of the Welsh economy — firms stayed as long as the costs were low enough. Wales was particularly attractive for advanced industry which handles basically semi-skilled assembly, and subsequently, is still relatively starved of more progressive functions, such as scientific research and development (Day 1986:165-166).

An analysis of electronic enterprises in Wales (Glyn Williams 1986:184-187) confirmed Day's view of the continuation of dependent develop-

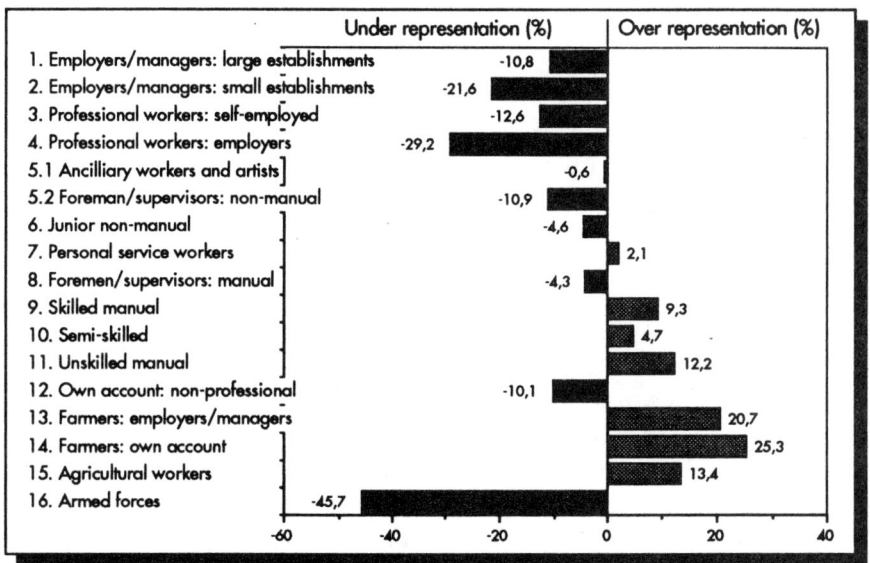

Fig. 4 Extent of over/under representation of Welsh-speakers in socioeconomic groups (Figures from Glyn Williams 1986:186, Figure 21).

ment. Two factors demonstrate the fact that the firms would have no difficulty relocating production when the relative advantage — subsidies, cheap labour, etc. — in Wales was lost: firstly, the training period for workers in these factories did not exceed two weeks, and secondly, there was a continuous shift in machinery. Furthermore, state intervention in a way perpetuated the uneven development by channeling public funds into private enterprises willing to invest in Wales. Williams assumed that "... such incentives were unnecessary since most firms were seeking advantages in terms of cheap labour and/or new markets." Moreover, they were dangerous for established enterprises which now had to compete with the beneficiaries of state subsidies — for many of the established enterprises the competition ended in liquidation. Economic restructuring has brought decentralized branch-plants and small firms to certain growth regions in the rural western and northern parts of the country. Another factor in the economic restructuring of these areas, besides the increase in manufacturing employment, was the rapid development of the tourist business. Williams argued that the evidence from the 1981 census in Gwynedd, a county with a high level of new developments of branch plants and manufacturing industries, supported the cultural division of labour thesis (see page 75). He compared the socioeconomic status of Welsh-speakers and of people born outside Wales and found a heavy over-representation of non-Welsh born in the top four socioeconomic groups and an over-representation of Welsh-speakers in the lower socioeconomic groups (Fig. 4). "There seems to be little room for capital accumulation by indigenous, non-oligarchic entrepreneurs. The data merely show an acceleration of the tendency for most industry in Wales to be non-Welsh owned." (Glyn Williams 1986:187)

The economic restructuring of the Welsh economy had profound implications for Welsh society. In spite of the cultural division of labour, a rising number of Welshmen succeeded in acquiring middle class jobs within the education system, the civil service, and the universities. Khleif (1978:104) argued that the new post-war intelligentsia consciously used Welsh ethnic identity as a tool for creating a sense of distinctiveness in the competition with other groups. Welshness (primarily defined through the ability to speak the language) provided the new Welsh middle class with a secure boundary and clear-cut criteria for distinction in the competition with other groups (basically the Anglo-Welsh middle class) for the same status position. "Ths [sic] Welsh-speaking intelligentsia, the 'most conscious and awakened part of the middle-class' (Smith, 1981: 37), one with a sense of historic grievance and, hence, of heightened ethnic identity, has made its own socio-economic and socio-political interests synonymous with those of all of Wales; it has refused to compromise on the issue of language, thus losing the support of Anglo-Welshmen, that is, of non-Welsh speakers ..." (Khleif 1984:4). Even though Khleif seemed to identify with the ideology of the Welsh-speaking intelligentsia, his description of the development of the new Welsh middle class was not without merit. However, he was apparently too preoccupied with the Welsh middle class view and overlooked the internal conflict between the Welsh working and middle class which the language movement has created (in this context Welsh means the Welsh-speaking *Cymry Cymraeg* (Welsh Welshmen)). Furthermore, the emphasis of the Welsh middle class on language has widened the gap between the Welsh and Anglo-Welsh in Wales. The historically rooted divisions and contradictions of Welsh society have certainly been one reason for the rejection of limited autonomy by the majority of the Welsh people in the devolution referendum in 1979.

8 COFIA TRYWERYN![36]

THE ANTHROPOLOGY OF RURAL COMMUNITIES IN WALES AND THE DISCOURSE OF WELSHNESS

In his contribution to the devolution debate John Osmond (1978:11) wrote: "If there is one thing that unifies the people of Wales who, considering their relatively small number are amazingly diverse, it is their preoccupation with locality and community. They are an abiding theme in the work of Welsh writers, both in Welsh and in English. Point of origin is practically the first information exchanged when any Welsh people meet. Wales boasts hundreds of celebrated communities and though, of course, there is no unanimity on their order of rank, nothing could be calculated to unite Welsh people more than to threaten any one of them. The most infamous modern instance was the drowning of Tryweryn in Merionydd." Even though this is clearly a political statement, perpetuating the ideas of "romantic" Welsh nationalism, the fact that the Welsh community of Capel Celyn in the Tryweryn valley had to make way for a new reservoir, which was exclusively build for the water-supply of new industry in the Merseyside area, by the Liverpool Corporation in the late 1950s, is still used by many Welshmen (in 1989) to demonstrate the fatal effects of the English central states' policies for Welsh communities. The Tryweryn project, once again revealed the powerlessness of local or other authorities in Wales, which, of course, aroused much anger in Wales. The Welsh poet R. S. Thomas (cited in Sager 1985:419) has expressed this in his poem "Reservoirs":

There are places in Wales I don't go:
Revervoirs that are the subconscious
Of a people, troubled far down
With gravestones, chapels, villages even;
The serenity of their expression
Revolts me, it is a pose
For strangers, a watercolour's appeal

To the mass, instead of the poem's
Harsher conditions. There are the hills,
Too; gardens gone under the scum
Of the forests; and the smashed faces
Of the farms with the stone trickle
Of their tears down the hills' side.
Where can I go, then, from the smell

---

[36] „Remember Tryweryn" was a slogan painted on many walls throughout the countryside after the drowning of Capel Celyn.

Of decay, from the putrefying of a dead
Nation? I have walked the shore
For an hour and seen English
Scavenging among the remains
Of our culture, covering the sand
Like the tide and, with the roughness
Of the tide, elbowing our language
Into the grave that we have dug for it.

R. S. Thomas, "Reservoirs" (cited in Sager 1985:419)

Plaid Cymru benefitted from the controversy because the "... emotive appeal of preserving rural Welsh communities, and also of conserving 'Welsh water' for local benefit rather than have it transferred free of charge to English cities, had clear nationalistic implications." (Morgan 1982:382) Despite its nationalistic implications, the construction of reservoirs for the benefit of English cities was, Morgan (1982:335) argued, really more a rural-urban conflict than a Welsh-English one. I doubt that it is possible to distinguish clearly between a rural-urban and a Welsh-English component because in the predominantly rural areas in North Wales the rural-urban conflict seems to be conceptualized essentially as a Welsh-English conflict.

Tryweryn remains an open wound — in the dry summer of 1989, when there was very little water left in the reservoir (called Llyn Celyn) and the ruins of Capel Celyn were clearly visible, almost every Welshman in the area made a bitter remark about the destruction of the community and its people by the English centre. In times of intensive social change and a perceived threat to the Welsh community, Tryweryn is used, particularly in the rural areas of North Wales, as, what Cohen (see page 54) has called, a "condensation symbol" which is mythically infused with timelessness and heavily charged with emotions. The use of the symbol is a means of strengthening the ethnic boundary. However, the meaning of this boundary for the Welsh people may be largely imperceptible to those from outside. Cohen (1985a:13) argued that the unfavourable outcome of the 1979 devolution referendum was due to a misinterpretation of the meaning certain boundaries had for the people concerned. The Labour Government assumed "... that there was sufficient unanimity of attitude within ... [Scotland and Wales] ... to give particular legal expression to their boundaries." (Ibid.) But the argument went much further than the simple question whether power should or should not be devolved to new authorities. Rather, the people within Welsh and Scottish communities started to "... question whether the boundaries envisaged by Whitehall were the most salient to them." (Ibid.) The problem was not simply couched in terms of the England-Wales/Scotland dichotomy but also in terms of intra-Welsh/Scottish differences — in regard to Wales this meant, Welsh versus Anglo-

Welsh, north-western ethnic traditionalists versus south-eastern modernizers, etc. . I believe that in Wales, the question which became suddenly prominent was, whether the boundary dividing Wales from England was more meaningful to the Welsh-speaking Welshman form North Wales than the boundary dividing him from the English-speaking Welshman from South Wales — and further down the scale: whether it was more meaningful than the boundary dividing the people from Porthmadog from those of Blaenau Ffestiniog. Cohen argued that as one goes down the scale the " 'objective' referents" of the boundary become less and less perceptible for the outsider but more important to the members of these entities "... for they relate to increasingly intimate areas of their lives or refer to more substantial areas of their identities." (Ibid.) I would argue that the failure of the referendum was, at least partly, due to a misunderstanding by the central government and an ideological blindness by the nationalist parties of the implications this new set of boundaries would have had for the inhabitants of, say, Porthmadog or Caerdydd (Cardiff). Cohen's description of the reasons for the failure of the devolution referendum in Scotland and Wales, even though it provided a valuable insight into the problem from the perspective of the local community which has too often been ignored, is, however, too preoccupied with the local or community level. A major weakness of Cohen's assumption lies in the lumping together of Scotland and Wales regardless of the different historical and societal conditions. The importance of construction of identity at the community level should not be underestimated, for it can provide us with a useful starting point for the understanding of current social and political processes within Wales, Scotland *and* Britain as a whole. That the community studies revival in social anthropology had virtually no effect on research in Wales is even more surprising, if we consider the great importance of the idea of community in Wales, for its members' perceptions of themselves, and for the construction of their identity.

Some sociologists in Wales, however, have rediscovered community studies as an idea worth considering. In his programmatic article on the issues and prospect of the sociology of Wales Graham Day (1986:173) wrote: "The growing recognition that many of the questions about the interaction of different social variables can be resolved best through the study of their workings within particular localities has also produced a renewal of interest in the community study style of work, in which Welsh sociologists once played such a leading role, even if such research carried out now would be built upon very different theoretical and value assumptions."

During the 1950s Welsh geographers indeed played a leading role in the study of rural communities in the United Kingdom. Two years after the publication of Arensberg's study on rural communities in the west of Ireland in 1937 (Arensberg 1968), the Welshman Alwyn D. Rees, University Extra-Mural Tutor of the Department of Geography and Anthropology of the University College of Wales at Aberystwyth, embarked upon a similar fieldwork of a rural community in north-east Wales (Llanfihangel yng Ngwynfa, Powys). The idea of undertaking research into contemporary Welsh culture emerged in 1938 during discussions between Rees, Professor Ifor L. Evans, the Principal of the University College, and Daryll Forde, who was Gregynog Professor of Geography and Anthropology at Aberystwyth. Originally a series of community studies was planned, but with the outbreak of war the work was delayed (Rees 1950:v). After the war the work was continued by post-graduate research students whose studies were published in abbreviated form in a volume called "Welsh Rural Communities" (Davies & Rees 1960)[37]. However, after the highly productive phase of the immediate post-war years the short life of the Aberystwyth School came to an end in the mid-1950s when the joint Department of Geography and Anthropology shifted its focus to the study of geography (Glyn Williams 1986:177). Nevertheless, "... they established a community studies tradition that has shaped many subsequent analyses and studies of communities in Britain." (Glyn Williams 1978:2). The first of the anthropological studies of rural communities in Britain was Alwyn D. Rees' study of the parish of Llanfihangel yng Ngwynfa in Powys.

Llanfihangel yng Ngwynfa ◀

When Alwyn D. Rees embarked upon his study of the parish of Llanfihangel, he had no particular methodological approach in mind. Nevertheless, his work "... was essentially an attempt to adapt the approach of the anthropologist to the study of contemporary Welsh life." (Owen 1986:94) It is not surprising, therefore, that he tried to find a manageable unit which, in accordance with the functionalist paradigm of the time, could be studied as a whole. He found his manageable unit in the parish of Llanfihangel

---

[37] Another student of Rees, W. M. Williams, did research in the English rural communities of Gosforth and Ashworthy (W. M. Williams 1956, 1963).

which lies near the English border. In 1940 the parish had a population of 500 of which 90% lived in scattered farmsteads, and the remaining 10% in the three small hamlets of Llanfihangel, Dolanog and Pontllogel. Like so many rural areas in Wales the parish has suffered from a steady population decline since the mid-nineteenth century (Rees 1950:11-16). Rees chose this parish "... partly for reasons of convenience and partly because it is a relatively secluded and entirely Welsh-speaking area which could be expected to have retained many features of the traditional way of life." (Ibid.:v) Like Arensberg & Kimball (see chapter 2) Rees believed that the community he had chosen represented a kind of microcosm of society. He wrote: "I believe that in spite of its proximity to the English Border, the social organisation of the area remains fairly representative of the Welsh uplands in general ..." (Ibid.:v). The empirical data were gathered through participant observation, interviews and questionnaires completed by every household in the parish. In addition to these methods of data collection, he also used census data, and consulted historical documents concerning the parish. Unlike the vast majority of social anthropologists, Rees not only gathered data on culture and social structure, he also was very interested in material culture. Two chapters (III and IV) of his monographs are devoted to house types — farm houses are classified into two broad categories of older "oblong type" houses and newer "square type" houses — and their internal layouts, and the layout of farmsteads. The whole book resonates with Rees' interest in Celtic folklore and the philosophies of a Welsh nationalism (see pages 81-82) that saw the values of Welsh "civilization" embedded in the medieval Welsh society. Consequently, history plays an important part in his analysis — most notably when cultural differences between England and Wales are explained. This is evident in Rees' discussion of the family and the kinship system.

The family is seen as the primary social group and the unit of economic production. The economy was based on agriculture and to a very high degree dependant on the English economy. All finished goods, except foodstuff, were imported from England, and as a result the material culture retained little that was distinctive. Even though the standard of living was generally low, the farmers were not inclined to forsake their traditional occupation. Rees (1950:31) claimed that family solidarity, kinship bonds, the belonging to a religious denomination, and the status the individual has achieved in the community, would tie the farmer to his locality and would make it impossible for him to live elsewhere. Furthermore, Rees

(1950:60, emphasis added) argued, that "... the family farm is the *basic institution* of the Welsh countryside." Ideally, the farm is run by the farmer and his family, however, when the children are still too small for farm work or when most of them have married, the farmer has to rely on hired labour. Most of the hired labour was provided by other families who had a surplus, so that some of the older children were free to work elsewhere. As a result, most of the farmers had at one time been farm labourers. Thus the employment of farm labour operated within the family farm system. Rees described the relationship between the farmer and his employees as traditionally reciprocal, analogous to the relationships between members of the family working on the farm. Working hours are not defined and there are no recognized holidays, on the other hand, the farm labourer is not expected to work on rainy days and is looked after by the family in case of illness. However, when the Agricultural Wages Board prescribed a 48 hour week in winter, a 52 hour week in summer and payment for overtime, a conflict arose between (Welsh) custom and official (English) regulations (Rees 1950:61-62). Rees saw this as the imposition of urban (which is synonymous for English) standards and claimed that "... many farmers complain that there is not the same interest and pride in work as in the old days." (Rees 1950:62) While the older sons usually went to work on other farms and saved their wages to provide for the purchase of a farm when they married, the youngest son usually stayed at home and inherited the farm. He could not marry while one of his brothers was still at home or while his mother lived, and thus the age of marriage was considerably higher than it was in Britain generally. Regardless of age, the son which remained on the family farm could only become a full adult member of the community through marriage. Rees had the impression that "psychological effects of this prolonged boyhood" were the reason for reticent and subdued behaviour as well as a certain degree of immaturity. On the other hand, the economic dependence is not resented because wealth is seen as a family possession which will be shared out at marriage (Rees 1950:63-66).

The budget of the farmer's wife was largely independent from that of her husband. Her income derived from the sale of domestic produce. Rees argued that the role of the farmer's wife in the 1940s was comparable to the role of the wife of a freeman in medieval Welsh law (Rees 1950:63). But not only the role of the farmer's wife was seen as having its roots in medieval Welsh society, Rees assumed that many of the customs he had described were rooted in the social system of medieval Wales. The fact that the Welsh farmer retained control of the land of his kindred until his death was contrasted to the practice of the English farmer who often gave his holding to his successor during his own life-time. Another feature of the medieval and the contemporary system of inheritance was the fact that the sons were entitled to equal shares of moveable property and, after the death of the father, also to equal shares of land. The farm, the remaining land, and the movable property were reserved for the youngest son. Rees concluded: "Although the old tribal society has long since passed away, something of its spirit lives on in the cohesion and paternalism of the present-day family. This survival has been ensured by the hereditary nature of the farmer's craft." (Rees 1950:72)

Until marriage or until a man became a confirmed bachelor, the young men of Llanfihangel were part of the "youth group". They were referred to as *y bechgyn* (the boys) or *y llanciau* (the lads). The members of this "youth group" were between 16 and 35 years old and most of them had well passed their youth. Obviously, the designation "youth group" refers to the inferior, non-adult status which unmarried men have in the community, rather than to their physical age (Rees 1950:82-84). Emrys Lloyd Peters (1972) — "Welshest of the Welsh" (Frankenberg 1990:180) at the Manchester department — has argued that youth groups in Welsh rural communities were important for the control of morality and the maintenance of the "moral community". The group meets regularly at the local shop in Llanfihangel, where they engage in a performance of making fun of passersby. Their behaviour has two significant aspects: on the one hand it is spontaneous and trivial like their remarks on passersby, on the other hand it takes the form of planed collective action against individuals who have violated certain moral norms. Another important aspect of their behaviour is the, sometimes violent, reaction against individuals and groups from outside the community who attempt to cross its boundary, which is in Peters' eyes "... emblematic of the unity of the community ..." (Peters 1972:115). Rees (1950:83) argued that the behaviour of the youth group is not as anti-social as it may seem and that the majority of the community secretly approved of it. However, Peters found it difficult to define the "community" within which the actions of the youth group could be understood. He assumed that there was "some sort of community" (1972:124) which was evident in the group consciousness of the youth group and found its expression in the hostility towards strangers and youth groups from other localities. The youth group acted in accordance with a consensus which directly related to the conception of the moral order by the adult community. Most spheres of morality were the domain of institutions (law, religion, family) which were controlled by the adult population. Peters describes them as of a more universal character and therefore as being too rigid to deal with complexities of daily life. The youth group, however, was more flexible and was able to respond to events which the institutions of morality could not comprehend in their local complexity (Peters 1972:123-124). As the social adults — according to the Welshman Emrys Lloyd Peters — see it: "The ignorance of immaturity gives the youth group the irresponsible freedom to act; maturity traps adults into the measured responsibility of inaction." (Peters 1972:135) By transferring responsibility to the youth group — which is external to the adult community in the sense that it is regarded as irresponsible and that its members have not yet matured to full social adulthood — the adult community can maintain an appearance of unity. Apparently the youth group is *re-*creating the public face of the (adult) community boundary, while at the same time mediating change and continuity. Peters (1972:130) argued that part of the importance of these youth groups in Wales derives from the fact that they mark the boundaries of a moral community, and thereby play an important part in the "knitting together of otherwise isolated nuclei". However, the youth group does not simply maintain the status quo, the established consensus of the adult community, but it also can create new meanings for adult customary behaviour.

In Llanfihangel, in contrast to "modern urban communities", kinship is said to pervade every sphere of life. In many parts of the parish every household is connected to every other by kinship ties. Kinship provides a very important category for the internal classification of individuals. Descendants of a common ancestor are often referred to as a group by the surname of the ancestor ("the Joneses" or "the Evanses"), or by the name of the farm which belonged to the ancestor. A certain status is also ascribed to people belonging to a common descent group. Kinsmen also serve as an emotional link to the past which is evident in the terms to describe these relations. A cousin is not called a cousin, rather he is referred to as my father's (mother's) sister's (brother's) child. Kinship solidarity plays an important part in the social relations of the community. Rees (1950:79-80) argued that the "... kindred has an organic quality; what happens to the individual is felt by the whole group." From this he assumed that the "clannishness" had two social functions. On the one hand, it gave the individual a sense of security and belonging, on the other hand it was a powerful means to control the behaviour of the members of the group (Rees 1950:73-80). Rees traced the kinship system of the 1940s back to medieval Welsh society. Kinship solidarity, he (1950:81) said, was a "... heritage from the tribal past. A tribal organisation of life continued in a modified form in Wales throughout the Middle Ages, in contrast to the feudal system of rural England."

Kinship constituted only one pattern in the "intricate social fabric" of Welsh rural society. In the rural upland areas of Wales kinship groups are scattered over a wider geographical area, and, therefore, social relationships which are based on close physical proximity play an important part. Rees argued that social relationships between neighbours were particularly important because isolation was imposed on the inhabitants of upland areas by the environment. Isolation and the lack of any central place could only be overcome by close contact with one's neighbours which could provide companionship and cooperation — before the advent of modern agricultural machinery cooperation was absolutely necessary, and in the 1940s the main cooperative tasks were reduced to threshing, sheep-dipping and shearing. With which neighbours a farmer cooperates is determined by local custom and each farm is the centre of a cooperative network. These networks overlap, and thus the whole parish is covered by a "continuous network of reciprocities", which cuts across boundaries of class and kinship. Cooperative activities have not only a practical value, rather they are important social events. The lavishness of hospitality is crucial for the families' and the kin groups' prestige. Rees argued that the cooperative networks are a distinct feature of Welsh society derived from the structure of medieval Welsh society. He called it a "diffused form of society" without a unifying social centre which was opposed to all forms of centralization (Rees 1950:91-99). "The farms are not outlying members of a nucleated community, but entities in themselves, and their integration into social groups depends upon the direct relationships between them rather than upon their convergence on a single centre. The traditional social unit does not consist of the environs of a town or village; it is *cefn gwlad*, the neighbourhood in the countryside." (Rees 1950:100) Furthermore, he argued that this is still evident in the peripatetic tradition of many cultural institutions, like the local and national *eisteddfodau*.

The *eisteddfod* plays an important part in the social system because success in the singing or poetry competition at the *eisteddfod* is a major source of prestige. Rees argued that social differentiation rested more on a distinct system of values which attached more importance on nonmaterial accomplishments than on class position. Class distinctions were described as comparatively weak because the division between farmers and wage-earners has been less definite. The comparatively low amount of capital needed to start farming in the upland areas made it possible for wage-earners to set up a farm. Rees assumed that a third of the farming families may have been wage-earners a generation ago. "Owing to this elasticity of the social system, kinship groups, although they vary considerably in their collective wealth and prestige, tend to cut across class boundaries, and even the richest families have some poor relatives." (Rees 1950:142) Another factor was that every family had roughly the same cultural and educational background — which basically meant that the vast majority had only received primary school education. The emphasis in Rees' account of status and prestige lay on the "Welsh way of life", which has "... not yet succumbed to the materialistic values of the modern world which tends to measure everything in terms of production and profit ...", as opposed to what he saw as the urban, materialistic, and, last but not least, English culture (Rees 1950:144). The Welsh system of ranking was seen as based on social status for which the main criteria were cultural achievements, all-round competence and skills, whereas, in England people were stratified in classes according to material wealth and economic power. However, with the establishment of a branch of the Farmers' Union in the late 1930s the old system was beginning to crumble and the alien form of solidarity, class solidarity, advanced from across the border. Rees vehemently proclaimed that this kind of unity, "... the rural counterpart of urban trade unionism ...", based on economic interest, remained unintegrated with traditional Welsh culture (Rees 1950:160-161). It will remain unintegrated because it "... lacks the vitality and idealism of Welsh Radicalism which appealed to people's sense of justice as well as to their self-interest, and invoked principles which could be expounded from the pulpit as well as in the market-place." (Rees 1950:161)

Finally, Rees tried to mask his unreflected preoccupation with the nationalist discourse of Welshness by saying that every "... ethnographic description is more or less selective ..." (Rees 1950:162), and by saying that he was only concerned with describing those features which distinguish Welsh rural culture from its English counterpart. His emphasis on history and the continuous reference to medieval Welsh society, in connection with his anti-urbanism, places Rees firmly in the tradition of the romantic nationalist discourse initiated by Saunders Lewis. It is, thus, not surprising that he assumed that the feature of Welsh society in the 1940s that was most distinctive, was "... an inheritance from the pastoral and tribal past. Greatly modified it persists in the high evaluation of family and kindred, in the hospitality extended to strangers and in the maintenance of a pattern of community life which is specially adapted to a scattered habitat." (Ibid.) In England, on the other hand, inheritance of land was impartible, kinship is weakly developed, and the social and economic life is centred in the village. As a consequence of the weak blood ties, English society assumed to have been well prepared for the social isolation of urban areas. In contrast to the English, the Welsh people were not prepared for the onslaught of the urban-industrial revolution. Rees saw three reasons why Welsh culture had not been able to withstand those outside influences. The first was a lack of a unifying vision for the whole society. Secondly, Wales suffered from a "brain-drain", which meant that the talented Welshman had to go to England to get on, thus, Wales was loosing its elite. Another factor which Rees saw as crucial to the decline of Welshness, and identity in the modern world in general, was mobility. He argued that the discontinuity of residence weakened the social influence of the Welsh elite which had remained at home. Thirdly, the effects of the industrial revolution were described not only as a great transformation of material culture of rural Wales, but also as "... highly disruptive to the social fabric in general ..." (Rees 1950:166). The old system which relied upon traditional reciprocity was replaced by a system of commercial relationships. Subsequently the people became alienated from their work and their kin and neighbours. Rees' conclusion resonates with the pessimism of nineteenth century writers like Durkheim and Tönnies. He envisaged Llanfihangel, and Welsh society in general, as being at the verge of "... social atomisation which is general in Western civilisation." (Rees 1950:168) For him, modern society had not only failed and was in a state of, what Durkheim would have called, *anomie*, but, worst of all, still tried to impose its values on a culture which had provided a better social order for its members. He wrote: "The failure of the urban world to give its inhabitants status and significance in a functioning society, and their consequent disintegration in to formless masses of rootless nonentities, should make us humble in planing a new life for the countryside. The completeness of the traditional rural society — involving the cohesion of family, kindred and neighbours — and its capacity to give the individual a sense of belonging, are phenomena that might well be pondered by all those who seek a better social order." (Rees 1950:170)

Welsh Rural Communities

The influence of Alwyn D. Rees is evident in the studies presented in the volume "Welsh Rural Communities" (Davies & Rees 1960) which was published in 1960. The authors of the four community studies — David Jenkins, Emrys Jones, T. Jones Hughes, and Trefor M. Owen — were all natives of rural Welsh communities, and Jenkins was, in fact, brought up in the community he studied. Nevertheless, Elwyn Davies and Alwyn D. Rees, in their editorial preface to the book, claimed that the authors were able to achieve a certain degree of detachment through their study of comparative anthropology and the fact that they had lived and worked elsewhere. "But, fundamentally, these are studies of a culture 'from within', the Welshman as he sees himself." (Davies & Rees 1960:xi) Davies and Rees claimed that the emphasis of all studies rested on the members' perception of Welsh culture in which, they assumed, "the essentials of the culture" could be found (Ibid.). Davies' and Rees' vague description is all that can be found on theoretical or methodological issues, for the individual authors did not disclose the theoretical background and the methods employed in their community studies. However, it is evident that the emphasis lay not on meaning and the perception of the community by its members but on structure. In accordance with the structural-functionalist paradigm, structure was seen as determining behaviour.

The communities were studied for one or two years between 1945 and 1950 and were scattered throughout Wales. David Jenkins' study of the village of Aberporth in Dyfed and T. Jones Hughes' study of the village of Aberdaron and the surrounding parish in Gwynedd, were both studies of coastal villages which had experienced a profound economic change after the basis of their economies, shipping and fishing, declined during the late nineteenth and early twentieth century. Emrys Jones presented a study of the market town of Tregaron in Dyfed, whilst Trefor M. Owen's study was mainly concerned with the implications of Nonconformity for the life of the rural communities on the southern shore of the Llyn Tegid (Bala Lake) in Gwynedd.

T. Jones Hughes' (1960) contribution on the village of Aberdaron which lies on the western end of the Llyn peninsula is a social geographical study which is primarily concerned with the spatial distribution of material and non-material elements and tells us little about social relationships. The Llyn peninsula is a remote area on the western coast of Wales in which it was claimed, as Hughes (1960:123) informed us, that "... survivals, mainly of pre-industrial character [can be found], which are to-day regarded as the hallmarks of Welsh nationality and cultural separateness." The most impressive of these survivals is the Welsh language which was spoken by almost everybody in the area. Hughes argued that traditional Welsh culture survived in association with the Welsh language, and that the distribution of the language is an expression of social, economic and physical distance. Consequently, Aberdaron was chosen as the object of study because it could be regarded as a residual area (Hughes 1960:123).

Until the beginning of this century the economy of Aberdaron was based upon its functions as one of the most important small ports in the Llyn distributing provisions for the surrounding countryside and for inshore fishing. With the advent of large steamers and the improvements of the roads the port lost its role as a distribution centre. Inshore fishing also declined and the population suffered from a very high degree of unemployment. Farming in the area, was until the 1930s largely based on cattle breeding. During the 1930s milk production for the wider market was introduced to the Llyn and during the Second World War the demand for dairy produce increased dramatically. Liquid milk, that could be produced by most farmers, provided the first stable market for the Llyn farmers, and Hughes argued that the regular supply of money caused a rise in the standard of living, which "... is one of the most critical factors involved in the departure from the traditional way of life." (Hughes 1960:133) After the Second World War, Aberdaron recovered from the effects of unemployment and poverty during the inter-war years. Aberdaron, like the whole of Llyn, developed into a secluded holiday resort for the English and tourism quickly became the most lucrative source of income. Furthermore, Aberdaron developed into a service-centre providing shops, a bank and post-office, and medical care for the surrounding countryside.

Even though the divisions of the parish in terms of geographical divisions in land tenure and religious affiliation, etc. are examined in great detail and historical context, the social implications of these divisions are only superficially analyzed or, more often then not, not analyzed at all.

Instead, very much like Rees, he indulged in a lengthy discussion of house types and their internal layout.

Emrys Jones' (1960) study of the market town of Tregaron has in some respects certain parallels with T. Jones Hughes' study of Aberdaron. He also emphasized the spatial division of the neighbourhoods in the community. Tregaron was divided into five neighbourhoods: the Square, Pentref, Doldre, Chapel Street, and Station Road. Originally the village was confined to the *treflan* (small town) around the church and Pentref, an agglomeration of houses centred around the mill. From the thirteenth century Tregaron gained the right to hold an annual fair which developed into one of the most important fairs in Wales. By the mid-nineteenth century Tregaron had become a centre of cattle trade because of its advantageous geographical position on the road leading to the English cattle markets. A new neighbourhood around Chapel Street emerged. When a new road to Llanbedr Pont Steffan (Lampeter) was built in the late 1830s the river Brennig was canalized and the Dôl (meadow) was now free from floods and was quickly settled. The growth of Doldre was connected with the growth of the hosiery trade and wool manufacture. With the coming of the railway in 1866 the town expanded towards the station and a new neighbourhood around Station Road developed. During this phase the wool industry declined and Tregaron's function was once again that of a market town. In the twentieth century the town developed into an administrative and service centre for the surrounding countryside.

Tregaron's function as a service centre is also evident in the occupational structure of the town. Jones divided the population into three status classes. Class 1, 45% of the employed persons, held administrative, professional, managerial and proprietorial occupations; class 2, 15% of the employed persons, were craftsmen or specialized workers; class 3, 39.5%, were unskilled workers and labourers. Members of class 1 live in Station Road, Chapel Street and the Square, members of class 2 and 3 in both, Pentref and Doldre. Jones argued that the occupational structure of Tregaron in the early 1950s was the result of nineteenth century changes which led to the determining role of occupations in the structure of Welsh rural society. The rise of the middle class is a key factor in this development because the middle class took over the leadership in the society and was dependent on the recognition of the new class order. The growth of the Nonconformist chapels, which coincided with the development of the stratification system based on occupational classes, strengthened the position of the middle class, when the chapels coupled themselves with the new order. Jones assumed that the system of status group ranking was imposed by forces from outside the community, and, therefore, as having no relationship with indigenous Welsh society. However, the new stratification system did not destroy the older system, rather it added an additional layer to it. He argued, that classes in Tregaron were not as exclusive as similar classes in "... a thoroughly urban culture ..." (Jones 1960:90). The small size of the community (the population in 1946 was 609), the frequent face-to-face interaction between members of different classes, chapel membership, and the important role of kinship ties reduced the consequences of class divisions in the community. Religion, which means membership of a Nonconformist denomination, is described as a pervasive element in the social life of the community, furthermore, it is also a decisive factor in the assessment of individual status. The observance of religious rules, such as strict Sabbatarianism, and wealth — the status hierarchy based on occupation is recognized in the chapel — are the basis for respectability which is the prerequisite for high status in the community. Kinship bonds are more important than class divisions. Family and kinship relationships play an important role in the social structure of the community, they "... permeate every aspect of life in this closely integrated society ..." (Jones 1960:92) and "... weld the society into a whole of which each individual is an integral part." (Jones 1960:114) Like his colleagues of the Aberystwyth School he sees the close social relationships of the Welsh rural community — which he traces back to medieval Welsh society — in contrast to the isolation which characterizes urban communities. In Tregaron most families were connected by kinship ties and the obligations arising from those ties are highly valued. "All these attitudes reveal the vestigial remains of the closely knit kinship groups of medieval Welsh society." (Jones 1960:92) Outside the kinship groups, Jones stated, the whole community is united by a feeling of belonging to the locality. The primary division in Tregaron is that between those who belong — the local people with kinship ties — and those who do not belong — newcomers without kinship ties. Close relations between kinship groups and the encompassing feeling of belonging to the locality are the factors which make "... Tregaron a single entity, so difficult for the native to disassociate himself from, and so difficult for any stranger to identify with." (Jones 1960:99)

---

38 The parishes Llanuwchllyn and Llyngywer. For reasons of convenience Owen used the name Glan-Llyn for the whole area. Two-thirds of the inhabitants of the two

In contrast to the other studies in "Welsh Rural Communities", Trefor M. Owen's (1960) study of Glan-Llyn[38] dealt with a single aspect of community life, the chapels. Owen's aim was the description and analysis of social activities in the community which were centred upon the fifteen Nonconformist chapels (one chapel for every sixty-three inhabitants) in the area in 1949. Like Rees, Owen saw the family as the primary social group and the unit of economic production; the economy was based on the family farm. The system of employment of external labourers operated along the same lines as in Llanfihangel, and a third of the farmers had at one time been employed as farm labourers with relatives or neighbours. Owen argued that this system "... has served to minimize the distinctions between servants and employers and to preserve the homogeneity of the community." (Owen 1960:188) Family and kinship relationships pervade the whole community life, they are the most important social relationships. Besides the close kinship network, the social relationships based on neighbourliness are of prime importance for the social system of the community. Kinship and neighbourhood ties provide the basis for cooperative activities on the farms (sheep shearing and threshing) as well as social activities. As a result of the massive depopulation of the Welsh countryside kinship provides not only an internal system of social relationships but also provides for contacts with the outside world. Another important link to the outside world are the market towns of Bala and Dolgellau. Changes, in the form of technological innovations, a higher standard of living and higher mobility, had not disrupted the stability of the community in the late 1940s. Owen assumed that the intensity of kinship and neighbourhood ties, face-to-face interaction in the community and the unifying effect of chapel activities, had provided "... an effective barrier to the permeation of city ways." (Owen 1960:189) 94.4% of the population were Welsh-speakers and the only language of the social and religious sphere was Welsh. Religious and social life was dominated by two Nonconformist denominations, the Congregationalists and the Presbyterians. For Owen the question arose, why these Nonconformist chapels, which very decisively had turned their backs on worldly affairs, dominated the institutional social life of the community. To gain insight into this phenomenon he presented an account along historical and structural lines.

---

parishes (676 out of 948 in 1951) lived in houses owned by the Glan-Llyn estate.

Owen argued that the success of the religious revivals in the eighteenth and nineteenth century was partly due to the way in which the Nonconformist sects attached themselves to the traditional social habits and used them for their own purposes. In the eighteenth and nineteenth century knitting provided some extra income for the farmers of the area. In winter the *noson weu* (knitting night), where neighbours met to knit and chat in one of the farmhouses, was the centre of social life. Since the mid-eighteenth century Nonconformist preachers had used these *noson weu* to propagate their religion, and so nonconformism was brought to every farmhouse. However, with the spread of puritanical nonconformism many old traditions were abandoned because they came to be regarded as corrupt and immoral — the social life of the community was almost in its entirety reduced to the observance of religious pursuits. Public entertainment, such as the *twmpath chwarae* (cock-fight) and the *gwylmabsant* (saint's festival — which had an almost purely recreational character and little religious significance), were destroyed by puritanism and the home became the only place were entertainment was permitted. When nonconformism had established a firm hold chapels were built throughout the countryside and the religious meetings on the farms were discontinued; consequently the number of religious meetings and the religious awareness decreased. Owen assumed that the building of the chapels had a detrimental effect on the religious activities because they were no longer located at the centre of everyday life, and, therefore, declined to a peripheral weekly experience. However, this change had a wider significance because the secular activities of the home were also transferred to the chapel. When puritanism lost its power, the distinction between the chapel and the outside world became less clear-cut, and entertainment, of the type that had been practiced in the farmhouses, again became permissible. This, Owen argued, provides insight into the question why the secular life developed not independently, but as an integral part of chapel life. Through this "secularization" the chapels gained a controlling position over the religious as well as the social life of the community. "The chapel congregation as a group has maintained its strong position in the face of a declining religious consciousness by reinforcing the religious motives for belonging to it with the more mundane desire to participate in the formal recreation it offers to its members." (Owen 1960:218)

The structural aspects of religious organization for the community were analyzed in comparison to the structure of a Hebridean community that

Owen had studied. In regard to the religious organization the Hebridean community resembled the Glan-Llyn of the early nineteenth century. In the Hebrides the sacred and the secular were clearly separated and secular entertainment remained wholly outside the control of the chapel. In Glan-Llyn the situation was markedly different. The kinship system and the religious system were inseparably connected. Despite the fact that nonconformism stressed the personal responsibility of the individual to work out his own salvation, it became customary for the members of the same family to belong to the same sect. The importance of kinship and neighbourhood ties and the division of the secular life along denominational lines resulted in a high degree of denominational endogamy. Owen (1960:230) wrote, that to "... the individual belonging to a particular congregation in effect means participating in a particular social system ...". The Nonconformist chapel influenced the social ranking in the community in two ways. Firstly, the Christian ethic was translated into the language of everyday life. Ideals of neighbourliness, hospitality, obligations to one's family were framed in terms of religious duties. Secondly, a high status within the congregation was carried over into public life. The persons who had a high prestige in the chapel also became leaders in other spheres of social life. The significant division was that between the different denominations. In the Hebrides the significant division was that between members and adherents because unlike Glan-Llyn, where all members of a congregation were real members, only the profoundly religious adherents were admitted to the higher religious status of a member. The basic difference between Glan-Llyn and the Hebridean community was, that in Glan-Llyn the significant differentiation was along vertical lines and in the Hebrides along horizontal lines. For Owen, vertical differentiation meant that several parallel social systems existed which were modelled along the same lines and had a balanced pattern of relationships covering both secular and sacred activities. In the Hebridean community these vertical lines were less significant because of the strict division between the sacred and the secular spheres of community life. Instead, the horizontal lines — the relationships between individuals of the same religious status — were far more important and cut across the vertically oriented social systems.

In the coastal village of Aberporth, David Jenkins (1960) found a horizontal status group division similar to that in Owen's Hebridean community. The area Jenkins had studied contained three distinguishable social neighbourhoods, pentre Aberporth, Parc-Llyn and the surrounding farming area which were interconnected by kinship ties. During the nineteenth and twentieth century the economy was based on fishing and the shipping trade. Aberporth had not suffered from the economic changes of the late nineteenth century. The inhabitants which were well established in the small ships trade turned their attention to large shipping companies — two large companies were founded by Aberporth families. Thus, at a time when most inland villages suffered from emigration, the employment provided by the shipping trade ensured the continuity of the community. Furthermore, Aberporth had developed into a small holiday resort which attracted English families, and some of them came to stay permanently in the community. During and after the Second World War an army camp and the Ministry of Supply Research Establishment brought a large number of English people into the community. However, in 1949 the community was still almost entirely Welsh-speaking (525 out of 684, over 80%, of the inhabitants spoke Welsh). Out-migration of the younger people to seek work elsewhere was a fairly recent phenomenon in the late 1940s. It was connected with a decline of the shipping trade and the availability of secondary education. With the decline of fishing and the shipping trade Aberporth developed more and more into a service-centre for the surrounding countryside.

Kinship categories are essential for placing or knowing of people. The main distinction is that between the *pobol Aberporth* (Aberporth people) or *pobol y lle* (people of the place) and the *pobol dwad* (nobody's people — strangers). Jenkins, as a native to the community, claimed that the importance of kinship is evident in the fact that *pobol* (people) is most frequently employed to express the status of an individual. The term *pobol* can be used for people in general, however, most of the time it is synonymous with kinship group. Without any *pobol* to whom the individual belongs, he/she is totally isolated. Furthermore, Jenkins argued that the application of the term *pobol* to kinship groups and to the community as a whole expressed "... attitudes which in this society are 'natural', usual, customary, basic, and unconsciously adopted." (Jenkins 1960:11) Neighbourliness, together with kinship, is presented as a traditional cultural feature of the Welsh rural community. Neighbours were bound together by reciprocal relationships in the form of customary obligations.

Jenkins argued that the term *pobol* is indicative of an important social category in the indigenous classification system. The imposition of class categories would lead us to ignore the different perception of significant divisions in the community by its members. Classification in terms of upper, middle, and lower classes "... would be largely unreal, unrecognized in the speech and behaviour of the local people. The only terms in Welsh for upper, middle and lower classes are translations from the English; they are scarcely known to most, and never used by any, of the indigenous people of the area." (Jenkins 1960:13) The two most significant categories in the internal discourse of the community are, on the one hand, the *pobol y dafarn* (pub people) and the *bois y pop* (pop boys), and on the other hand, the *pobol y capel* (chapel people)[39]. In order to describe these two groups Jenkins employed the terms *buchedd A* and *buchedd B* — *buchedd* can be translated as "way of life", or "life-style"; it denotes morally adequate behaviour (cf. Owen 1986:11). He argued that the division between *buchedd A* and *buchedd B* was more significant than the economic, occupational, or cultural divisions within the community. Members of *buchedd A* were described as strict adherents to the religious rules, they were sabbatarian and teetotallers, and as thrifty people — "thrift" described the attitudes towards spending money, rather than income. Education and knowledge were respected for their own sake and because education meant a chance to "get on in the world". *Buchedd B* people were almost the exact opposite of *buchedd A* people. They were not sabbatarian, frequently went for a drink to the pub, and were more ready to spend money on immediate pleasures. Kinship is a factor which influences the *buchedd* differentiation. Another factor is occupation, especially the differentiation of high prestige intellectual work and low prestige manual work. Jenkins constructed four groups according to *buchedd* status and occupation. The *bucheddau* were correlated with two occupational groups: group 1 consisted of teachers, lawyers, doctors, Merchant Navy Officers, nurses and bank clerks, group 2 of labourers, mechanics, farm hands and shopkeepers.

(1) *Buchedd A* and group 1 occupation — 35% of *buchedd A*: People in this group attend service regularly, do not break the Sabbath and are teetotalers.
(2) *Buchedd A* and group 2 occupation — 65% of *buchedd A*: They hold religious offices (Sunday School teachers, deacons) and their children are given the best possible education.

(3) *Buchedd B* and group 1 occupation — 4% of *buchedd B*: This group is very small because the pursuit of prestige occupations is the result of *buchedd A* values.

---

39 Jenkins differentiated the chapel people into two groups, the *pobol y seiet* (people of the [religious] society) and the *pobol y cwrdd* (people of the [religious] meeting).

(4) *Buchedd B* and group 2 occupation — 96% of *buchedd B*: People in this group rarely attend service, drink and are not sabbatarian.

Jenkins assumed that the second group (*buchedd A* and occupation 2) is probably the most characteristic group, furthermore, it "... is the group upon which any attempt to base a social classification on occupation alone breaks down, for it is only as a sub-group of the *buchedd* structure that it finds its right place." (Jenkins 1960:17) The emphasis placed on education and achievement by the members of buchedd A had some serious consequences for the social structure of the community. First of all, Jenkins pointed out, secondary education did not serve the needs of the local Welsh community. The curriculum was standardized, dominated by the values of "English" culture and industrial society in general. As a result it alienated the school children from the local Welsh culture. Furthermore, the scarcity of high prestige occupations forced the educated members of *buchedd A* to emigrate. Thus, the "brain-drain" was not simply the consequence of economic pressures, rather, Jenkins argued, it was the result of the values held by the *buchedd A* group. The values system of the *bucheddau* contributes to emigration in yet another way. Because of the high degree of social control people are either forced to leave the community or conform to its values. As a result, many young people, especially from *buchedd A*, emigrated. "The buchedd A ideology, one might say, contained the seeds of its own impoverishment, if not of its own destruction." (Owen 1986:113)

The dichotomy, that Jenkins described as the *buchedd A-buchedd B* dichotomy, originated in the religious experience of the Nonconformist revivals. The chapels produced a distinct society of believers within the community who kept themselves aloof from worldly matters. The *bucheddau* as the significant categories of internal differentiation, which transcended class distinctions, emerged and were generally accepted when nonconformism began to dominate the life of Welsh communities. Nonconformism was to a great extent free from the direct influences of the English or Anglicized gentry, and the absence of the gentry from *seiet* (religious society) and chapel meant that a status system independent from the imposed values of the dominating class could be established. In Jenkins' view, the *buchedd* system submerged distinctions based on other grounds, such as occupation and class, though it did not totally negate them. "While the members of the lower class differentiated among themselves and the gentry, *y pobol fawr* [the big people], they also differentiated among themselves, and in the Nonconformist chapels they created a status system in which the gentry had little or no part. Indeed the social change which had taken place could hardly have come about without the effect on the attribution of status." (Jenkins 1960:53) Jenkins suggested that his *buchedd A* group was the much secularized modern descendant of the believers and that his *buchedd B* group represented the people more concerned with "worldly" matters.

As we have seen, the contradistinction of English and Welsh culture played an important part in the work of the indigenous Aberystwyth School. This is not surprising since the members of the School were all native Welshmen, which were participating in a certain discourse of Welsh identity that was based on a heightened awareness of cultural distinctiveness, anti-English and anti-urban sentiments, and the search for the roots of Welsh society in a tribal past. It was the assumed historical continuity of family and community from tribal past to "colonial" present that lead to a perpetuation of the myth of the family farm as a focal point of Welshness. The use of history by the Aberystwyth School also echoes Arensberg and Kimball's (1968:xxxi) assumption that Irish society has a "... relatively unbroken tradition dating back to pre-Christian and pre-Roman times ...". The concept of the family farm as the basic institution of the countryside reminds one of Arensberg and Kimball's notion of family and community as the basic — and therefore enduring or static — institutions of human association. Rees argued that the spirit of the old tribal society lived on in the cohesion and paternalism of the modern farm family. However Gibbon (1973:490), who criticized Arensberg and Kimball's assumption of the immense deep-rootedness of the patriarchal order, has shown that the legitimacy of paternalism in rural south-west Ireland was shallow and fragile. The discussion of inheritance, late marriage and "prolonged boyhood" is also part of the construct of the patriarchal order. Whether the psychological effects of "prolonged boyhood" and in some cases the prospect of never having the chance to marry were only expressed in subdued behaviour and a degree of immaturity, as Rees wants us to believe, is questionable. The phenomenon of "prolonged boyhood" was also described by Arensberg and Kimball (1968:55-56) as a characteristic of the family farm system in the south-west of Ireland. Hugh Brody (1986), who did a re-study of the rural west of Ireland in the 1960s, gives a quite different account of the consequences of "prolonged boyhood". He described the bachelors as the potentially most disadvantaged and depressed group in the community. For him they are an expression of human demoralization in the countryside (Brody 1986:42-43). Human demoralization, however, is conceived as a sign for social change which has affected the Irish countryside since the time of Arensberg and Kimball's study in the late 1930s. Brody has been criticized by Gibbon (1973:491) for taking Arensberg and Kimball's description at face value. Gibbon argued that the changes which Brody described as novel were only novel in relation to the romantic account of rural society given by Arensberg and Kimball. Their "... functionalist theoretical position produced an account of the Lough which had more in common with the visions of obscurantist nativists and revivalists than with concrete reality. On every score — the family, the 'mutual aid' system, the economic and cultural stability of the system, and its politics — their account ranges from the inaccurate to the fictive." Gibbon on the other hand, argued that demoralization had been an acute problem of the Irish rural communities at the time of Arensberg and Kimball's study. In regard to Welsh rural communities in the 1950s, both Jenkins (1960:31-32) and Jones (1960:78) have shown that inferior status of the heir, even as a middle aged man, economic dependence of the sons on the father, and the lack of paid wages for family labour were incentives to move away from the family farm, either to establish a new farm or to work elsewhere. The potentially disruptive effects of inheritance and prolonged submission to paternal authority on the social relations of the members of a farm family in changing rural societies is a widespread phenomenon. These changes have also very likely affected Welsh rural society especially after the second World War. The contact with the wider society increased considerably through improved infrastructure and mobility, the mass media, etc., leading to the introduction of new ideas to rural communities. Rural depopulation continued on a relatively high level and as Mewett (1988) has shown, out-migration — for more than purely economic reasons — can develop into a normative aspect of social life. In Welsh society which places such a high value on a good education, and "getting on", out-migration is certainly a kind of normative, but contradictory, aspect of social life. Furthermore, due to the availability of alternatives and the increasing devaluation of the farmer status, the sons of farmers will no longer be willing to endure the psychological effects of prolonged boyhood. This has been clearly shown by Davydd Greenwood (1976) in his study of the Basque community of Fuenterrabia. The conflicts created by the prolonged inferior status of the heir and the total submission to paternal authority until the death of the father, were only tolerated as long as there were no attractive alternatives to a farming life and being the heir to a farm was connected with a certain prestige in the community. However, with the decline in the prestige of agriculture (despite the fact that farming was a profitable business) and the increasing independence of young people the old conflicts were brought into the open. Such a process has certainly affected the rural communities described by Rees and the Aberystwyth School. Emmett's (1978) in her study of Blaenau Ffestiniog boys (see pages 136-139) is a good example for the struggle of the youths for their rights to more independence in the 1960s.

Many Welsh social scientists have been absorbed by the powerful discourse of Welsh identity. Community and language are the two key issues in this discourse which originated in the ideology of Welsh cultural nationalism of the 1920s (see page). The situation of Welsh communities, and the state of Welsh society in general, was, and is still, conceptualized in terms of a romantic *Gemeinschaft-Gesellschaft* dichotomy which very closely resembles that of Tönnies. A serious problem in the community studies of the Aberystwyth School is the lack of critical reflection which resulted, firstly, in a confusion of indigenous ideal-models and analytical constructs by the anthropologists, and secondly, in a confusion of ideologically based constructs with reality. David Michael (1983:34) criticized the Welsh intelligentsia, especially the social "scientists", which had created a new cultural consciousness, as narrow-minded anti-modernists, interpreting every modernizing impulse as a betrayal of the native culture. The Aberystwyth School was seen as having produced a cultural division within Welsh sociology that had isolated it of from the mainstream of sociological thought. Alwyn D. Rees, in particular, was characterized as "... the last great ideologue of a decadent Welsh weltanschauung [sic!] ..." (Michael 1983:34, emphasis removed), perpetuating the myth of a society of *gwerin* that presented Wales as a classless society of poor but proud, religious, and highly civilized people. However, Michael seriously underestimated the value the community studies undertaken by Rees and his students can have for our understanding of Welsh culture despite their sometimes ideologically biased analyses. In contrast to Michael, Glyn Williams (1978:2) suggested that the community studies of the Aberystwyth School contained

"... important analytical contributions and suggestions for further research." Moreover, he argued that the Aberystwyth School has been "... the only academic tradition in Wales with an institutional and unified basis for social scientific studies specifically on aspects of the social structure of Wales." (Ibid.) Even though the various authors did not explicitly state their theoretical approach it is quite clear that they all worked with a structural-functional framework. The deficiencies of this framework outlined in chapter 2 apply also to the studies of the Aberystwyth School. Yet there is probably a very specific reason why structural-functionalism has appealed to social "scientists" studying Welsh communities. In the discourse of Welsh ethnic identity, that was fostered by the intelligentsia, the concept of community as a "natural" unit, a closed system, was crucial for the understanding and construction of Welsh ethnicity. Thus, the structural-functionalist paradigm of the community as a functional unit, a closed system, a whole, corresponded neatly to the conceptualization of the Welsh rural community by the intellectual elite. Closely connected with the ideal of the Welsh community is the postulate of a different internal system of differentiation not based on class divisions. Class was seen as a concept imposed upon Welsh society by the dominant English society, threatening the culturally distinctive traditional social structure of the Welsh community. Stratification in the Welsh rural communities was described as being based on non-material criteria, such as kinship, religiousness and education. It was assumed, as in the case of Jenkins' *bucheddau*, that even though Welsh society was intertwined with the wider British society, the traditional system of stratification was still more important than any alien form of class system. Jenkins' *buchedd*-system attracted much interest as an alternative indigenous stratification system, but the fact that the *buchedd* categories were apparently an analytical construct invented by David Jenkins, rather than indigenous categories was largely ignored — in his description of the categories the members of the community employed to differentiate among themselves *buchedd* is never mentioned. The *buchedd* system was seen as having a much wider significance. Elwyn Davies and Alwyn D. Rees (1960:x) believed it to be the system representing the fundamental social division characteristic of all Welsh rural communities. Minchinton, Plowman and Stacey (1962:176) accepted the Welsh status systems as both local and customary, representing an indigenous Welsh culture. They and Frankenberg (see page 23) used the Welsh studies to support their notion of total status. They assumed that class differentiation, and status ranking corresponded in the internal stratification system of Welsh communities. Frankenberg (1969:58) also believed that the class homogeneity of Llanfihangel was maintained by emigration. Higher class positions were not available within the community, and people who wanted to achieve a higher class status had to leave the community. However, Frankenberg took no notice of the *buchedd* system.

Graham Day and Martin Fitton (1975), on the other hand, have criticized Jenkins' *buchedd* concept. They believed that the *buchedd* system as a stratification system which was based on status rather than class was not only built upon insufficient data, but reproduced the distorted members' perception of class relations[40]. The *buchedd* system "... has been built on the slenderest of foundations, and involves unproven assumptions, inadequate delineation of causal linkages, along with terminology and measures which are so idiosyncratic as to make evaluation of the underlying theory extremely difficult." (Day & Fitton 1975:867) They argued that class relationships in small communities, even though they may be masked by direct interaction which can conceal and mitigate differences in economic position, are still the most significant social relationships. Of all social phenomena, class is seen as the most crucial determinant, and thus, Day and Fitton expected that other criteria of social differentiation could, in the end, always be traced back to the "basic class order". For them, an independent culturally distinct system of stratification, not primarily based on class, was impossible. If there really was a different perception of class differences in a Welsh community, it could only be the result of the false consciousness of its members. It is not surprising, therefore, that their criticism of the Welsh community studies emphasizes the lack of information on class factors. Although their class bias has prevented them from seeing the possible cultural distinctiveness of the Welsh stratification system, they have uncovered some serious flaws in Jenkins' *buchedd* concept by questioning Jenkins' assumption of incongruence between class and status ranking, and of the consensual nature of the *buchedd* system. They examined firstly, whether status groups corresponded to occupational categories, secondly, whether interaction took place across occupational lines, and thirdly, whether leadership roles were monopolized by particular occupational grades.

---

40 Day and Fitton had access to Jenkins's unpublished M. Sc. thesis about Aberporth which contained more detailed information than the abbreviated version published in "Welsh Rural Communities".

A reconstruction of the occupational structure of Aberporth in the 1950s seemed to confirm Jenkins' assumption of incongruence between *buchedd* and occupational categories because the working class population was evenly split between the two *bucheddau*. However, Day and Fitton argued, when Jenkins' crude occupational division between non-manual (group I) and manual (group II) occupations[41] is examined in more detail, *buchedd* and occupational categories can be seen to overlap. A differentiation between skilled and unskilled jobs within Jenkins' group II showed that 60% of the skilled compared to 30% of the unskilled workers were to be found in *buchedd A*.

Day and Fitton's attempt to examine the interaction across occupational groups within the *bucheddau* from the minimal data Jenkins had recorded is far from conclusive or convincing. Even though Day and Fitton had to admit that it would be helpful to know more about the nature and strength of association between members of the different *bucheddau*, they tried to map the degree of interaction. Given the paucity of the data on the nature of the relationships involved in the interactions, such a simple counting of interactions between members of the different *bucheddau* will lead us nowhere. Their assessment of leadership and occupational status, however, is more solidly argued. Leadership is most clearly visible in the composition of the diaconate of the chapels, and that indicates a convergence of occupation and social status. The evidence for this comes form Aberporth (Jenkins), Tregaron (Jones) and Llanfihangel yng Ngwynfa (Rees). Of the 26 chapel offices in Aberporth, 19 are occupied by members of the high ranking occupation group and only 7 by manual workers. In Tregaron the most important places in the chapel hierarchy are occupied by members of the farming community and Jones' class 1, and the leaders of Llanfihangel are also elected from among the wealthy. However, this argument is simply superfluous as a criticism of Jenkins' *buchedd* concept because Jenkins never denied that a convergence of occupation and social status existed. As Glyn Williams (1983:145) has pointed out, Jenkins merely denied that a *necessary* correlation existed between them. Furthermore, Jenkins had only claimed that the *buchedd* system made it possible for those with low occupational status to acquire high social status.

---

41 A quarter of the 250 members of the community in employment held non-manual prestige occupations, the remaining three quarters had manual jobs.

In all studies of Welsh rural communities by the Aberystwyth School, religion plays an important part in the analysis of Welsh society. Day and Fitton claimed that there is general agreement about the role nonconformity played in the development of Welsh society on three points. Firstly, nonconformity played a leading role in the class conflicts between the gentry and their subordinates; secondly, the allegiance to the chapels was an additional way of distinction between the Welsh-speaking, economically subjugated, lower class and the English-speaking Anglican elite of landowners; and thirdly, nonconformity united the Welsh population. Jenkins argued that nonconformity had imposed a new pattern of social differentiation — the *bucheddau*, which were secular descendants of the religious division between the *believers* and *those of the world* — on a previously classless society. Day and Fitton, however, argued that the evidence pointed to a continuous adjustment of religiously based distinctions to the (occupational) class structure[42], and not vice versa. Furthermore, the evidence for the establishment of a new set of social distinctions as a result of the religious revivals is not sufficient. The distinction between believers and more "worldly" oriented people remained a theological distinction because the vast majority of the population were members of a congregation and many people "of the world" attended services and held important positions in the chapels. Thus the religious revivals seemed to have united the people, rather than having introduced a new social distinction.

Another argument against the diffusion of class conflicts is related to the production and reproduction of ideology. The dominant class must ensure that the key positions for the production and reproduction of ideology remain firmly in the hands of the elite, for the ideology which prescribes their supremacy is likely to be challenged in terms of the ideology itself, if non-elite members would be allowed to take key positions. The assumption that the *buchedd* system is a consensual system was repudiated by Day and Fitton because the *buchedd* system was not a system of mutual rights and obligations and the members of *buchedd A* felt no responsibility for those of *buchedd B*. They also expected that the system would break down when religious adherence declined and the members of *buchedd B* would repudiate the values which confined them to an inferior position. Subsequently, the members of the *buchedd A* elite would be forced to find new means of legitimation. Here, Day and Fitton's criticism is particularly weak because,

---

42 This point was also made by Emrys Jones (see pages 99-100).

in contrast to Jenkins, they presented the *buchedd* system as being unconnected with other systems, such as systems of kinship and neighbourhood, which are central for the social organization of the Welsh rural community. Unfortunately, Jenkins did not present sufficient data on the interrelation of kinship and *buchedd* groups, so that we cannot assess how they might be interconnected. Nevertheless, it seems likely, considering the pervasiveness of kinship, that the *buchedd* groups were part of a system of mutual rights and obligations which transcended class divisions. To isolate the status groups, represented by Jenkins' analytical construct of the *buchedd*, from the other systems of social organization would be as misleading as the ignorance of the effects the wider British class system must have had on Welsh society. Glyn Williams has criticized Day and Fitton for their simplistic criticism of the *buchedd* concept. He argued (Glyn Williams 1983:144) that the " 'poor but deserving' ethos" of the chapel was part of a tendency to deny economic rank, but did not alter the distribution of power implicit in the division of labour. However, he believed that the power relationships could be influenced by the ideology, so that in some contexts the power aspects of interaction would be negated, and some sense of equality generated. His most convincing argument was that the construction of equality was "... assisted by an equation of the religious code with ethnicity, Welshness being defined in terms of the cohesion of the status group and the integrity of allegiance to the moral code which served to define the status group." (Ibid.) Thus, ethnic identity cuts across class lines and channels the possible intra-group economic conflicts to the more obviously privileged gentry, which was defined as an "ethnic out-group" — the English. Those Welsh who aligned themselves with the so-defined English were similarly denied a Welsh identity. "Such an explanation has the advantage of integrating the interests of both parties [both *bucheddau*] within ethnic movement enhancing the interests of the leaders while also being aimed at improving the lot of the economically poorer ethnic cohorts." (Ibid.)

To postulate, like Day and Fitton did, that class is the most crucial determinant is by no means a better argument than to postulate, like many Welsh "anthropologists" did, that status is the most crucial determinant. This notion of mutual exclusiveness of stratification systems is highly unproductive. I would argue that a more productive approach lies in between the two approaches. Welsh society can be better understood as a complex system of interconnected stratification systems which are competing with each other. The denial of class categories for personal categorization within a Welsh community is not the outcome of *false consciousness*, it is more the expression of a culturally distinct system of stratification that, although increasingly influenced by the class order, has retained some autonomy because it is rooted within Welsh ethnicity and is important for conceptualization of the English-Welsh conflict. Day and Fitton however, attributed the existence of a culturally distinct system of stratification to the involvement and attachment — as opposed to the detachment the sociologist should exhibit — of the native anthropologist. "Whatever the general value of 'insider' status for research, it is obviously, and especially where there is a concern for the maintenance of a community, productive of its own biases." (Day & Fitton 1975:888-889) In contrast to Day and Fitton, I do not believe that the existence or significance of a culturally distinct system of stratification is only the result of a biased view of Welsh culture by the native anthropologist. Furthermore, that Jenkins' description of the stratification system of Aberporth is biased cannot automatically mean that the system is not existent or of no significance. "While Jenkins does fail to adequately develop the 'buchedd' argument and while Day and Fitton do succeed in uncovering some inelegancies in Jenkins' argument, their own attempt to fit the data into their own conceptual scheme hardly serves to resolve the issue." (Glyn Williams 1983:146)

9 STRANGERS AND PARTISANS

ENGLISH ANTHROPOLOGISTS IN NORTH WALES

Two English anthropologists, Isabel Emmett and Ronald Frankenberg, have also contributed to the study of rural communities in North Wales. Although, Emmett worked with basically the same structural-functionalist framework as her Welsh colleagues, her approach to the study of communities in the Welsh cultural context is notably different to that of the indigenous Aberystwyth School. The theoretical background to Ronald Frankenberg's study differed from both Emmett's and the Aberystwyth School's approach. Frankenberg, as an "aspiring Marxist" (Frankenberg 1990a:183), had developed an approach that was to a great extent derived from the theoretical considerations of Max Gluckman and the Manchester School. Both Emmett and Frankenberg were criticized by their Welsh predecessors. In their preface to "Welsh Rural Communities" Davies and Rees (1960:xi) stated that the outsider-anthropologist may find many features of the Welsh community inaccessible, and that "... the facets which he observes most readily are those which the Welsh student would regard as peripheral." Ronald Frankenberg's (1957)[43] study, "Village on the Border", is cited as an example for the study of parts of the social life in the community (the football club, the carnival committee and local government) which were regarded as peripheral by them. Nevertheless, they concluded that both, internal and external, viewpoints are relevant to the understanding of Welsh culture.

Frankenberg's (1957) study of the community of Glyn Ceiriog in Clwyd is mainly concerned with social processes involving power, politics and the structure of institutions. The fact that these processes were part of a Welsh

---

43 "Village on the Border" was first published in 1957. A reprint including Ronald Frankenberg's critical assessment of the original study appeared in 1990. The original study will be cited as Frankenberg 1957, the articles added to the 1990 reprint as Frankenberg 1990.

cultural context seems to have been purely accidental and of no special significance. In the 1957 edition we were not told why Frankenberg had chosen a *Welsh* community to study problems of conflict and cohesion in industrial society. It was only 33 years later (Frankenberg 1990) that he, in an article for the reprint of his study, gave an account of the events which had lead to the choice of a Welsh community as his fieldwork location. The circumstances which forced him to abandon his initial project, the study of "Unemployment and Family Structure in a West Indian Island" (Frankenberg 1990:171), were symptomatic for the experience that many anthropologists, for various reasons, had to face in the following decades: he was declared a *persona non grata* and was deported shortly after his arrival. In retrospect, Frankenberg also connects the misfortunes of himself as a young anthropologist with the development of anthropology. "To use modern terms, the discourse required not that I personally should come home but that anthropology should." (Frankenberg 1990:166) On return to England he was informed that he could only keep his field research grant provided that he worked within a day's journey from Manchester and under close supervision from Max Gluckman.

From the fact that "Glyn Ceiriog was not typical of rural Wales...", Owen (1986:115) derived the assumption that the selection of a representative community had not been Frankenberg's intention. However, Owen's interpretation of Frankenberg's intentions was too simplistic, for Frankenberg saw the community as a microcosm, containing the basic elements of the wider society which he made explicit in "Communities in Britain": "The Ceiriog valley is a microcosm, if not of Wales as a whole, at least of the north." (Frankenberg 1969:88) The problem of the microcosm model leads to another serious flaw of Frankenberg's study. The focus of his analysis on the study of social situations which occurred in several of the community's social institutions led him to believe that "basic values" of the community were "readily understood" (Frankenberg 1957:148). Frankenberg may have been tempted to take the basic values of the community for granted because he analyzed the situation of Glyn Ceiriog (as he wrote in 1990: "anticipating Hechter") as an openly colonialist situation in transition. He thought of the community as being similar to a "decayed island colony" whose resources had been exploited by foreign capital, and which had since been left overpopulated and without internal means of livelihood. In more general terms, he believed that all working class units in British society possessed the characteristics of a colonial society in transition (Frankenberg 1990: 180-181).

However, these generalizations were a misconception, for he was only able to participate in a very limited part of the social life of the community (he admitted that he was persuaded by his colleagues, mostly by the Welshman Emrys Lloyd Peters, that the description of Wales in terms of an "openly colonialist situation" was too crude a view). Most of the culturally distinctive features of the locality would have been accessible only through participation in that part of the social life of the community which was a domain of the Welsh language. It thus comes as no surprise that he was accused by Alwyn Rees of having failed to understand the essence of Glyn Ceiriog because of his non-Welshness and his inadequate command of the language (Frankenberg 1990:177). His role as an anthropologist was further complicated by the fact that he, as an Englishman, was deliberately excluded — by the Welsh-speaking members of the community — from those social activities where Welsh was spoken, although he was able to speak the language. He described Welsh as a "weapon of exclusion" (Frankenberg 1957:33). "During my own experience of 'Celtic' fieldwork in rural Wales, I and other Welsh-speaking English found ourselves excluded by language switches away from Welsh and into English at our approach ..." (Frankenberg 1986:342). From the scarce information he gave in the 1957 edition on his position in the community we can only deduce that he was classified as an outsider and therefore very likely to have been denied access to the Welsh part of social life. An incident which he describes in his reappraisal of the original study in 1990 clearly reveals his position, as well as his "... inadequate depth of immersion in the experience, the language, and the material." (Frankenberg 1990:184) His German-sounding name lead the villagers to suspect that he was a German spy, and this, accidentally, led to an improvement of his standing in the community when the police came to ask why he had not registered as an alien. That he was regarded with hostile suspicion by the authorities changed the attitudes of the villagers towards him — it made him "almost a Welshman in the eyes of many villagers" (Frankenberg 1990:175). However, it indicates his "ignorance" (or his preoccupation with structural similarities) of the cultural distinctiveness of the locality that he did not seek to understand the reason for this change of attitude towards him. He admitted that he learned that the police were resented as a representative of ruling England years later from Emmett's account of Llanfrothen (Ibid.).

Isabel Emmett (1964) who studied the parish of Llanfrothen, which she referred to as Llan, in Merionydd, described her problems in gaining access, especially the handicap of being English, more openly. The fact that she had married a local Welshman from Llanfrothen, which meant that she had kinship ties, however, only partially made up for her being an Englishwoman. She lived in Llanfrothen for 4 years (1958-1962) and after an interlude of 11 years in Manchester went to live in Blaenau Ffestiniog in 1973. In her article on Blaenau, published in "Belonging" (Cohen 1982a) she admitted that her inability to speak Welsh had been "a severe handicap" (Emmett 1982a:165). Indeed, this is a severe handicap, for the study of the peoples' perceptions and conceptualizations of their community and culture in Welsh-speaking Wales, David Jenkins (1980:125) argued, is impossible without a thorough knowledge of the language. "And one wonders what can be the aim or value of any study of a community or society unless it concerns itself with those concepts."

The English anthropologists undertaking fieldwork in a Welsh community had to face certain problems which have certainly affected their ethnographic accounts. Due to the historically rooted tensions between the Welsh and the English, English anthropologists wanting to analyze Welsh culture were certainly viewed with some suspicion. Like the English immigrants they were excluded from social activities which were regarded as central to Welsh culture within a rural community, since these activities were perceived as being threatened by the encroachment of English society on the Welsh community. In this sense, then, Davies and Rees may have been right in saying that many features of the Welsh community were inaccessible to the outsider-anthropologist, and that many features which the outsider-anthropologist describes would be regard as peripheral by the native anthropologist.

Glyn Ceiriog

The village of Glyn Ceiriog, for which Frankenberg used the pseudonym Pentrediwaith (literally: village without work), is located in the county Clwyd only a few miles from the border. The name Pentrediwaith pointed to the most serious problem the community had to face, the economic decline of the area. At the time of his field research most of the men had to work outside the parish in England. The settlement structure of the parish is the typical outcome of the growth of the slate industry in North Wales in the early nineteenth century. Frankenberg (1957:25-26) quoted a history of the Industrial Revolution in North Wales by A. H. Dodd who had shown how rapidly the mining villages (e.g. Bethesda, Llanberis and Ffestiniog) grew after the repeal of the slate duty. The economic crisis of the inter-war years had totally disrupted the economy of the parish. The slate quarries began a slow decline in the 1920s and were closed just before the Second World War. Farming was also affected and many farms in the area, so near the English border, were bought by Englishmen. Consequently, the parish suffered from a high rate of unemployment which forced the men to seek work in England.

It is not surprising, considering his theoretical background (Manchester School, Marxism), that conflict is emphasized in his analysis of community life. The unit of analysis was defined, referring to Gluckman, by a social situation, or more precisely by a social drama. As Frankenberg (1982:11) explained, Gluckman had taught him to look at partial situations, chosen for typicality, in order to understand the total situation. The partial situation had the advantage of being a manageable unit for research into social relations in action that made up the culture of a community, while at the same time being representative of the total situation. The concept of the social drama, which he borrowed form V. W. Turner, was central to his analyses of the workings of committees in Glyn Ceiriog (Frankenberg 1966:143-148). The social drama, in Turner's sense, was an ideal vantage point from which the crucial principles of the social structure could be observed, for when the social norms were breached and a crisis arose the social structure became transparent, which was most of the time opacified by a regular, uneventful social life. Furthermore, to reduce or resolve the conflict, special social mechanisms were brought into play (Turner 1957:91-94). Thus, it seems to be quite logical that Frankenberg's description of the community emphasizes the divisions within it.

Frankenberg sought to establish the contradictory principles of social organization (Welsh vs. English descent, Welsh-speaking vs. English-speaking, Chapel vs. Church, working class vs. farmers, etc.). In his search for contradictions he had been inspired by the ideas of Marx, Mao Tse-Tung, and by the concepts which Max Gluckman (1968:63-64) had put forward in his "Analysis of a Social Situation in Modern Zululand". Gluckman argued that there is a dominant cleavage in any social system which is rooted in the fundamental conflict of the system (the cleavage between Whites and Zulu in Gluckman's case). In addition, there may be subsidiary cleavages in any part of the system operating along similar lines to those on the whole system. Frankenberg thus looked for the *principle contradiction* or *dominant cleavage* in the community and believed that he had found it in the interest of men and women. Women's interests where identified as a principle aspect of the principle contradiction (Frankenberg 1990:186).

The loss of local employment was the reason for major division in the social life of the village, for the men developed interests outside the community, while the women remained to a large extent tied to the community. Another, very fundamental, division of the community is the class division. This is historically connected with the ethnic division of the Welsh and the English, which is expressed by the Welsh inhabitants in the animosities against "ruling England". Frankenberg argued that the division along class lines was evident in the political institutions. While the County and Rural District Council were dominated by English-speaking, Anglican, salaried or self-employed people with no connection to community life, the Parish Council was recruited from among the Welsh-speaking, Nonconformist wage-earners which were connected with the community by kinship ties. Frankenberg saw Glyn Ceiriog as an "organic part of Welsh society" (Frankenberg 1957:11), a microcosm in which the social and economic class divisions of Wales were reflected. He described the villagers as of roughly the same economic class but divided by religious affiliation (Anglican Church or Nonconformist Chapel) and language. These "national" social class divisions were bridged in the community by innumerable formal and informal ties. Nevertheless, a latent hostility between the church and the chapel people remained which could, in times of crisis, turn into open conflict. The substance of the dispute became sometimes obscured when the conflict was transferred onto a different level where the social divisions within the community were expressed in terms of the more general Welsh-English hostilities. However, Frankenberg argued that a very marked feature of the community was the continuous attempts of its members to mask the mutual hostilities and avoid open, disruptive conflicts. The attempt to maintain the appearance of a unanimous, leaderless unity, by the avoidance of direct statements in public and the delay of requests which are disapproved, made the role of leaders very ambiguous. The people of Glyn Ceiriog are more prepared to accept decisions of outsiders and are very sensitive to any attempt of uppishness on the part of a fellow community member. "Glyn people are strongly egalitarian in outlook." (Frankenberg 1969:98)

Therefore, Frankenberg argued, *strangers* were chosen for leadership. Who was chosen to be the *stranger* depended upon the context. In a group, every person who deviated in some respect from the other members of the group could be defined as a *stranger*. When a conflict broke out and a decision had to be made which threatened the interests of one group, but which was nevertheless necessary, the *stranger* could be blamed. Thus, the unity of the community could be maintained in spite of serious conflict. "Social groupings maintain their own cohesion by bringing in a stranger both to act as a scapegoat and as a reminder to group members that they belong and must maintain their solidarity against others who do not." (Frankenberg 1957:98) Frankenberg regarded the scapegoat function of strangers as his contribution to Gluckman's concept of conflict and cohesion, for the *stranger*, by serving as a scapegoat, ensures the maintenance of the community's unity, and thus the return to a state of equilibrium. The notion of the *stranger*, however, was not a simple addendum to the concept of conflict and cohesion. As a Marxist, Frankenberg argued, he had to see the process in a more dialectical way. Each village activity increased the number of people which were dissatisfied with village activities. When the number of people grew it became a "mass", and this growing mass would at some point in the future of the community transform quantity into quality (or in the case of Glyn, lack of quality of life) and finally the village would cease to be a community (Frankenberg 1990:185)[44].

Gossip was also seen as a means by which conflicts could be avoided and a sense of community maintained. It enabled the members of the community to express their criticism without causing serious open conflicts. Outsiders, such as Frankenberg, were not allowed to gossip about Glyn Ceiriog people. The most crucial categories for interpersonal classification are those of *insiders* and *outsiders*. *Insiders* were defined by their kinship ties, chapel membership and their ability to speak Welsh. The *insider* group consisted mostly of shopkeepers, farmers and wage-earners. *Outsiders* were those people who lacked the characteristics of the insider group. They had no kinship ties in the community, went to the Anglican Church and were

---

44 For Gluckman (1963:49), Frankenberg's analysis was applied to a changing situation not one of repetitive equilibrium.

English-speaking or English by birth. They were not excluded from formal social life, for they provided most of the leading members of voluntary organizations (Frankenberg's *strangers*), but they were excluded from most informal social relationships and not allowed to take part in *insider* gossip. They did not belong because they could not be classified by reference to the familiar social groups — the closely knit kinship groups. The belief held by the villagers that everyone is related to everyone else helps to maintain the exclusiveness and unity of the community against the outside world. In Cohen's terms, we could say that it served as a symbolic marker of the community boundary. The close connection between the nonconformist congregation and the kinship group has been demonstrated by the anthropologists of the Aberystwyth School. Frankenberg regarded them not so much as religious organizations but as largely endogamous social groupings of extended kinship. The exclusiveness of the Welsh community was further increased by the feeling that external groups were a threat to the community's identity. The people of Glyn Ceiriog distrusted first of all English outsiders, but also people from South Wales and Welsh nationalists. Frankenberg (1957:77) assumed that the "...threat against their group identity from advancing English industrial power has engendered an opposition to all external groups."

The focus of Frankenberg's analysis lay on the workings of the committees concerned with recreational activities, such as the football club and the carnival committee, which he described in great detail. He argued that the football club served as a symbol of the community's unity and cohesion to the outside world. However, serious disputes between the male dominated football club and the equally important, female dominated football supporters' club broke out when the football club decided to move to a field outside the village and to bring in outsiders to play for Glyn Ceiriog. At the outset of the 1952-53 season the conflict between the two clubs was brought out into the open. The rift was deepened when the men failed to fulfil their reciprocal obligations to the supporters' club, like attending its whist drives. Reciprocity, Frankenberg argued, was an important factor for the maintenance of the community's unity, and when one group failed to fulfil its obligations serious conflicts were inevitable. As a result of this conflict, the supporters' club withdrew its support and its members continued their criticism from outside, and even worked actively against the interests of the football club. Finally, the withdrawal of support by the supporters' club led to the inevitable end of Glyn Ceiriog's football club in

1953-54. It seemed to Frankenberg that this kind of development was characteristic of Glyn Ceiriog institutions. The villagers tried to avoid conflicts, but once a conflict was openly admitted, the face-to-face nature of social relationships and the multiplicity of ties made its spread inevitable. In the end the community became so divided that the particular activity could not continue. In the case of the football club, football was replaced by a carnival.

Almost ten years later in his book "Communities in Britain", Frankenberg (1969:106) argued that where the members of a community were no longer bound by economic interests and religious ties into a cohesive unit, conflicts which were previously controlled by the need to maintain the community as a whole, would soon turn into "disruptive antagonism" and then into "apathetic indifference". This process would be accelerated by each successive failure of a social activity. Frankenberg (1969:106) suggested that "... each successive failure might decrease the cross-cutting ties of sentiment, positive and negative, which bind Glyn villagers into a community. If they were to find it no longer interesting to talk about each other, and if they were to have nothing left to quarrel about, the village would cease to be a community and would become a collection of dwellings housing, in chance proximity, some of the industrial workers of Britain. Whether in such circumstances new social ties would develop to restore lost social redundancy is one of the major questions of modern Britain."

A Community in the Port Talbot Area, South Wales ◀

Frankenberg had also studied another community in Wales with the same approach (social drama) as Glyn Ceiriog. A short account of a single problem which arose in the community was published in his article on "British Community Studies" in the ASA volume on the "Social Anthropology of Complex Society" (Frankenberg 1966:136-142). The problem he described was the conflict which arose when a "Welsh School" was introduced to a village community in the Port Talbot area in Glamorgan in 1954. The community was part of the South Wales Coalfield and had a population of about 2,000. In contrast to Glyn Ceiriog, Frankenberg assumed, that its boundaries were less clearly defined in geographical and economic, as well as social, terms.

Although the community was regarded as a very Welsh place (the majority of the population were Welsh-speakers), the attitude of its members to the Welsh language was different to that of the people of Glyn Ceiriog. Welsh was not used as a means to exclude English-speakers from the community. To avoid conflict, the groups with conflicting interests in the Welsh language avoided one another, and the dispute was thus prevented from turning into open conflict. However, when, as a consequence of the governments bilingual policy, one group wanted to start a school where their children would be taught in Welsh, they became conscious of the latent conflict they had avoided all the time. Both groups, opponents and supporters of the "Welsh School", saw the Welsh language as a valuable possession and agreed that the ability to speak Welsh was good for their children. Yet the ability to speak good English was seen as a necessary prerequisite for bettering one's economic status. Apparently, the villagers, even the Welsh-speaking ones, had an ambiguous, in a certain sense even contradictory, attitude towards the Welsh language. When the "Welsh School" was established it was not popular in the village and the villagers argued that the issue had split the community. Frankenberg argued that the nature of the village, the geographical and social segregation of the opposing groups, made it difficult for the conflict to become socially manifest. The only situation he observed where the conflict came into the open was the local *eisteddfod*, where the Baptist minister announced the children of the County Primary School as the *Parti Ysgol Saesneg* (English School Party). The headmaster of the County Primary School, whose own child attended the "Welsh School", was very annoyed and "... called out in Welsh, 'My school is not the English School, it's as Welsh as the other and it's been here longer'. The minister replied that he had meant nothing by calling it Ysgol Saesneg and if that was the sort of hostile spirit in which the proceedings were to be carried on, they might as well call it a day and go home." (Frankenberg 1966:142) The overt inter-group hostility revealed by this event, however, turned quickly into informal intra-group gossip. Interaction involving conflict across group boundaries took place only in formal terms in formal situations. Segregation of the different groups broke down only temporarily and the system was restored to a state of equilibrium.

LLANFROTHEN ◄

The second study of a Welsh community by an English anthropologist was Emmett's study of Llanfrothen. The parish of Llanfrothen lies in a part of

North Wales (on the border of the districts Dwyfor and Merionydd in the county Gwynedd) which was, and still is, predominantly Welsh speaking. Emmett mentioned that the inhabitants regarded other parts of Wales, where English was the dominant language, as not belonging to Wales at all. She assumed, that much of what she had said about Llanfrothen applied also to Welsh-speaking North Wales and particularly to Gwynedd. The parish had suffered from the decline of the slate quarries and the rapid depopulation which had affected almost every rural area in Wales. The population of the parish in 1959 was 346 (109 men, 132 women, and 105 children).

The parish was chosen as the unit of study because the villages were too small to contain representatives of all the groups she wanted to include in her study. The villages or hamlets included in the study where: Rhyd [Aber][45], where only four Welsh families remained; Garreg [Dinas], the centre of the parish where white-collar workers, some English people and manual workers lived; Tan-Lan [Pensarn], where only manual workers lived, and what she described as "… an untidy version of the undifferentiated community Llan people would like their whole community to be …" (Emmett 1964:xvii); last but not least, the sheep-farmer's village of Croesor [Carmel], "… which stands for the conscience and the tradition of the parish." (Emmett 1964:xix)

Isabel Emmett's study is notably different to Frankenberg's community studies. She was not so preoccupied with the functional aspects of social processes and therefore placed more emphasis on the people's perceptions of their community. Subsequently the community was not placed in some analytical framework. Her study is more idiosyncratic, in the sense that she focused on three phenomena which she found to be paradoxical and therefore significant. The first of these paradoxes was the apparent lack of class distinctions within the Welsh community in spite of its interconnectedness with the wider British society. The second paradox was salmon poaching, which had no apparent economic motive. Thirdly, the high degree of illegitimacy that existed in the community in spite of its strong condemnation by the chapels caught her attention.

In the analysis of the first paradox she identified two opposing systems of stratification, which were, however, closely interconnected. She called

---

45 Emmett found it necessary to disguise the names of people, villages and the parish and made up new names. Here the authentic place-names are used, followed by Emmett's names in parentheses.

these systems the Welsh and the English "prestige ladders". The "English" system was part of the wider British class system, in which occupational status and economic class were the significant means of classification. The Welsh prestige ladder was described as a totally different system. The significant criterion for the placing of individuals on this ladder was the concept of Welshness. Welshness was conceptualized in terms of what was conceived as culturally distinct values. Emmett (1964:12) argued that the "... Welsh value system is a relatively coherent mixture of chapel and all which the chapel is against, but which is Welsh." Unfortunately, what Emmett meant by Welshness remained diffuse throughout the book. The concept of Welshness, as conceived by Emmett, seemed to embody the feeling of belonging to a community, the awareness of its history, the ability to speak the native language, having a working class status within the wider system and being religious (belonging to a nonconformist congregation). "Just as Welsh as religion is good singing, eloquence, skill in writing and reciting poetry, country craftsmanship, physical endurance, sex permissiveness before marriage, cunning and hypocrisy, and all these are part of the Welsh value system." (Emmett 1964:13) According to Emmett, Welshness was not only defined by a positive reference to Welsh values, but also by a conscious negation of everything what was thought to be part of the English way of life. She believed (Emmett 1964:22) that the "key to understanding Llan people ... is the anti-English feeling of Welsh-speaking people." This anti-English feeling was entrenched in the common historical experience of Welsh and English people. Emmett argued the lack of class divisions within Welsh society was due to the Anglicization of the Welsh gentry. As a result of this process, belonging to the upper and upper-middle ruling classes became synonymous with being English, and class conflicts are thus expressed in terms of ethnic differences. The most prominent stereotypes of the English — the English were conceived as being rich, snobbish, aloof, and simply lacking in understanding — became inseparably connected with the concept of "Ruling England". Despite the fact that most of the English people — intellectuals who settled permanently in the village or long-term tourists — in Llanfrothen fitted the stereotype, individual interethnic relationships could sometimes mitigate the strong anti-English feelings. However, these relationships could not totally negate the powerful anti-English feeling. Emmett showed that there were two levels of anti-English feeling, a mixed feeling towards individual Englishmen, and a "partisan" feeling towards "Ruling England".

The opposing English and Welsh status systems with their contradictory values were the cause of many personal conflicts. This was intensified by a feeling of inferiority on the side of those Welsh people whose linguistic abilities in English were limited. English, the language of the dominant society, was perceived as giving the speaker a certain superiority. "Speaking good English and being accredited with social superiority are closely connected." (Emmett 1964:33) However, Emmett found that the Welsh status system countermanded the awarding of prestige by virtue of occupation or linguistic ability. Both systems are mutually exclusive because the individual could not rise on the English prestige ladder without loosing his Welsh prestige. The degree to which the individual would be influenced by the Welsh status system depended on three factors: age, the place of work (in the community, or outside), and the local social environment (neighbourhood).

Age affected the attitude of the Welsh white-collar worker towards his/her position on the Welsh prestige ladder. The older men/women had little or no opportunity to rise on the English prestige ladder and, therefore, had much to loose if they rejected the values of the Welsh community and adopted English ones instead — "... to them Welshness is what counts ..." (Emmett 1964:35). The younger generation however, was more likely to be influenced by English culture through cinema, radio, etc. Furthermore, they had more opportunity to rise on the English prestige ladder and less to loose by doing so. A second factor, the place of work, was important because the white-collar worker, such as the headmaster of the local school, while working within the community were subject to the pressures within the community to conform to the Welsh system. Thirdly, the neighbourhood may influence the white-collar worker's choice in which system he/she wants to rise on the prestige ladder. "Each part of the parish has a tradition of its own, and the part of the parish in which a person lives affects his social position or social aspirations." (Emmett 1964:37)

However, the younger generation differed in its response to the opposing status systems. The young people of the parish were classified by Emmett into four groups according to their response to the opposing status systems. The first group was characterized as the group of opportunists. In this group the young people became anglicized because they wanted to be modern, and experienced little personal conflict in the process. The young people of the second group were either ignorant of the new ways or believed that they could not adapt to the different system. The people of the third group, which Emmett called the "true resisters", stayed at home and adhered to the Welsh ways because they did not want to betray their roots and exchange them for a rootless life in an alienated mass society. The last group, which Emmett called the "regretters", was made up of those people who had become anglicized because of their parents' or their own ambitions, but who felt that their Anglicization had been a betrayal of their own roots. They had great difficulties returning to their own Welsh group because their manners and speech differed from that of the local people. Emmett argued that people of this group became consciously Welsh and joined the nationalist movement. However, by their very conscious affiliation to the Welsh way of life, they were isolating themselves from it.

An important point in her analysis of the status system is the rejection of Jenkins' concept of the *bucheddau*. She could not discover a division of the Welsh population along *buchedd* lines. Those people within the parish who could be placed into *buchedd A* because they were religious, thrifty and teetotalers, however, did not conform to Jenkins' other *buchedd A* criteria. They did not value the chance to "get on in the world" to such a degree that they preferred their children to leave the community. Welshness was far more important, even if it meant missing the chance for high prestige jobs and good opportunities outside the community. The Welsh people of the community were united by a common feeling of Welshness, and a value system that contained both religious values and those elements which were condemned by the chapels. "In Llan, most of those who vote for the Plaid [*Plaid Cymru*] are regular chapel-goers and teetotallers: people who might be regarded as 'buchedd A' were it not that they prefer their sons to dig ditches rather than to leave Wales, and that they go poaching with the rest." (Emmett 1964:100)

Emmett also rejected Frankenberg's concept of the "stranger" as a scapegoat. She argued that the language difference was more prominent in Llanfrothen than it had been in Glyn Ceiriog, and that the Welsh language was still very strong in the parish. The people in Llanfrothen could afford to blame each other, for the community was not perceived as immediately threatened by the English people. Emmett believed that English people were chosen to lead organization, such as the Women's institute, for three different reasons. Firstly, the Welsh people were unfamiliar with the workings of such organization, secondly the organizations were part of the English status system; and thirdly it was not Welsh to put oneself forward. However, the scapegoat principle worked on a higher level — England and the English in general were blamed for the major ills of North Wales.

The second paradox, salmon poaching, was also related to the omnipresent English-Welsh antagonism. Emmett described the act of salmon poaching as a ritual which united the Welsh community. It was a war against the river bailiffs, the representatives of "Ruling England", which celebrated the values of Welshness. "Being Welsh is more important than saving salmon. The fact that the work of the river bailiffs is seen as simply the preservation of game fish for the pleasure of rich English people, and not at all for the advantage of the local working population, makes it possible for people to unite against them and this makes poaching particularly suitable as an activity which unite people as Welsh; unites them against these representatives of English rule; unites them in an anti-official war." (Emmett 1964:72) Generally speaking, the English humiliation of the Welsh speaking people created a kind of "partisan warfare", and it was against the moral code of the community not to cheat officials — they were perceived as the incarnation of "Ruling England" whether they were really English or not.

The high rate of illegitimacy, Emmett's third paradox, was seen as being related to a traditionally permissive attitude towards sexual matters and the reluctance of men to marry. She observed that the actual behaviour of the people was far removed from the way they were supposed to behave according to the chapel code. In a small community everyone knows about everyone else and, therefore, the people must pretend not to know half of what they do know about the others, in order for the others to "keep face". It was by this practice of "not knowing" that the people were able to live with their own violations of the moral code. "Not knowing" also played an important part in the collection of information for gossip. As in Glyn Ceiriog, gossip was an important feature of social life in the parish. To exchange or withhold gossip was a way of avoiding conflicts and maintaining a sense of community. "Gossip is the commodity which is exchanged most in country life: it is the currency of social relationships ..." (Emmett 1964: 117).

Emmett found that there existed three levels of "community spirit" for the members of the community. The first is the feeling of belonging to a village community, which, although weakened by the decline of economic interdependence, was still the strongest bond. The next level was the parish, which was the most important unit and whose population was bound by a strong kinship network. The last was the county (Gwynedd) level which became meaningful as a result of the changes of the industrial revolution. With the advent of the industrial revolution and the rise of the slate industry, many men began to work outside the community and the parish, and subsequently the boundaries shifted from the previous natural boundaries to new economic boundaries. The increasing number and greater relevance of personal contacts outside the community and the improved infrastructure turned the county into a meaningful unit. "Fairs and the eisteddfodau are the formal ceremonials of this widest community: overlapping groups of poachers are the informal means by which its male members are joined in a proud Welsh, anti-English feeling of community." (Emmett 1964:129) However, the improved infrastructure also brought Gwynedd into closer contact with England. This contact increased with the advent of mass media, first cinema and radio and later television. The economic crisis of the inter-war years, the decline of the slate industry, the affluence of the English capitalists, and the impoverishment of the Welsh farmers and the industrial proletariate contributed to a powerful feeling of injustice. Furthermore, the humiliating experience of denigration of the Welsh language and the attempt to impose the English language upon the Welsh-speaking population, combined with the feeling of injustice, made the people of North Wales conscious of themselves as a group threatened by the overwhelming power of the dominant English society.

In her analysis of the social life in the parish of Llanfrothen Emmett, in contrast to the other Welsh community studies, emphasized the English-Welsh antagonism. Within the community there existed two conflicting, or competing, status systems: the English or wider British system based on class and the Welsh system based on the values of the local Welsh culture. It was the Welsh system that unified the community, not at least in the resistance against social change in the form of what Emmett (1964:44) has called "Anglo-Americanization". In this sense, Emmett believed that her analysis of this resistance might have a wider significance for other parts of the world. Emmett further believed that the Welsh people took their strength from "their sense of being country people" as opposed to urban dwellers; "their sense of being ordinary people" as opposed to officials; "their sense of being working class people" as opposed to the upper classes (Emmett 1964:141). However, she found it hard to imagine how Welsh culture, with its emphasis on egalitarianism, could survive after the rise of a new middle class.

Blaenau Ffestiniog ◀

In 1978 and 1982 Isabel Emmett published three articles on the life of the Welsh industrial town of Blaenau Ffestiniog where she has lived as a housewife and mother since 1973. She described it as living in the community rather than studying it; her knowledge was shaped by chance and personal preference. Her accounts of the youth rebellion of the mid-1960s (Emmett 1978) and of the social life of a Welsh industrial community in general (Emmett 1982a, 1982b) are thus rather more impressionistic than other anthropological community studies (including her own study of Llanfrothen). However, to my knowledge, her articles are the only anthropological accounts of a community in North Wales in the 1970s.

In Emmett's opinion Blaenau Ffestiniog was particularly relevant because it is one of the largest predominantly Welsh-speaking industrial towns in Wales. Blaenau is a relatively new town which was built after the expansion of the slate quarries a few miles north of the small village of Ffestiniog, high up in the mountains of Merionydd, in the mid-nineteenth century. In the late nineteenth century Blaenau was an important centre of the Welsh slate industry, linked to the new port of Porthmadog by the narrow-gauge Ffestiniog Railway. The roofing slates from Blaenau were shipped from Porthmadog to places all over the world — Blaenau slate was used in the rebuilding of Hamburg after the great fire of 1842, when almost the whole inner city was destroyed. The slate industry in North Wales was at its peak at the end of the nineteenth century. After the end of the strike at the Penrhyn quarries in Bethesda (the strike lasted for three years from 1900 to 1903), and with the advent of the Great War in 1914, the slow but steady decline began (cf. Morgan 1981:124-125). "The big German trade which had begun after the great fire of Hamburg in 1840 [sic!], came to a dead stand ..." (Boyd 1975:187-188). At its peak the Welsh slate industry had employed about 17,000 men, of which by the 1970s only a few hundred remained (Glyn Williams 1980:171). Of Blaenau's eighteen quarries (in 1880) only two were still working in 1972 which employed only a few men (Morgan 1981:327). The quarrymen of Blaenau were "a unique community" (Sager 1985:372), solidly nonconformist with a passion for choral singing and at first solidly Liberal and then solidly Labour with a passion for serious discussions. During their tea-breaks they met to sing and discuss politics and other subjects. Emmett argued (1978:88) that, in spite of their serious interest in politics and their trade unionism their radicalism was limited by geographical and political isolation, religion, poverty and a sense of inferiority in relation to the English bosses. Although I doubt that the reasons stated by Emmett are sufficient to "explain" the lack of radicalism of the Blaenau quarrymen, it remains a fact that, in contrast to the Penrhyn and Dinorwic quarrymen, the workers of Blaenau were "relatively acquiescent and compliant" (Merfyn Jones 1980:207). Emmett also argued that there was no important distinction in life-style between the quarrymen and the small farmers and farm labourers — they went to the same chapels and were part of the same community and culture. Merfyn Jones (1980:207-208) however, painted a different picture of the relationships between the quarrymen and the rural, agrarian population. The quarrymen saw themselves as distinct from the rural population and the contrast between the two groups was manifest in the contempt the quarrymen had for the rural population which they referred to as sheep or pigs. "They dressed, ate and thought differently; in the election of 1885 the Blaenau Ffestiniog went so far as to stand their own independent Liberal candidate against the rural based machine." (Merfyn Jones 1980:207) Considering the discrepancies between Emmett's and Jones' accounts, Emmett's picture of the Welsh community in Blaenau seems to be a bit too harmonious. The scarcity of data on intra-Welsh conflicts is probably due to her exclusion from the Welsh community life. She wrote: "All non-Welsh-speakers living in the town, including me, are excluded from the mainstream of the Welsh community's life." (Emmett 1982b:214) Thus, it is not surprising that the emphasis of her accounts of Welsh community life lies on the conflict, in which she, as a non-Welsh-speaking Englishwoman, played an active part.

Like in her study of Llanfrothen her emphasis lies on, what she has called, the Welsh versus ruling England antagonism. Although Emmett believed that the major social division in the social structure of Wales was the ruling England/Welsh community division — a product of a colonial situation — she found that the persistence of a distinctive Welsh ethnicity was "... not one paradox but a continuing mystery." (Emmett 1982a:171) She stated that she had repeatedly discovered that life in Welsh-speaking north-west Wales was inextricably connected with the consciousness of Welsh ethnicity. Therefore, she assumed that one could only make sense of it "... in terms of a struggle which in many important manifestations is cultural ..." (Emmett 1982a:167). Many Welsh people believe that the future of Welsh culture and language is endangered because the institutions which have been crucial for the maintenance of Welsh ethnicity in the past, the chapels, the small family farms and the slate industry are declining — the quarrymen are seen as one of the chief custodians of Welsh culture and language. Furthermore, English culture is omnipresent in the media; Welsh people watch English television and read English newspapers, magazines and books. The problems for Welsh language and distinctive Welsh ethnicity are well known by ordinary Welsh people, however, they are far from being the central preoccupation. Nevertheless, Welshness is positively asserted daily in the interaction of the people within the community as well as in formal organizations, political parties and academic institutions. Emmett argued that the assertion of Welshness did not only involve the speaking of the language and the adherence to traditional institutions and practices, but also the recognition of the different meaning that "being Welsh" has for Welsh-speaking and non-Welsh-speaking Welsh people.

While a Welsh community was differentiated in cultural terms, she assumed that it was relatively undifferentiated in economic terms. Moreover, she also saw this as a common feature of Welsh inland communities in north-west Wales, presumably in contrast to the northern coastal areas of Gwynedd (from the border to Conwy) which are almost totally Anglicized, with a very large percentage of English incomers. However, "undifferentiated" did not mean that it was not related to class stratified society. Emmett argued that class may have appeared to be peripheral in some community studies because the ruling class was often distant, which made it invisible and faceless for the members of the community. In addition, class structure, like high level politics, is supra-national and not localized. The world of the powerful people in the community is thus centred elsewhere and their distancing from the community is reciprocated by it — in the past the enemy had been at least physically present. In this context it made special sense to Emmett that the class struggle manifested itself to a large extent in nationalism. Economic decisions were made in England, almost all industry, land and other productive wealth was concentrated in the hands of English or Anglicized landlords and English companies. The recent influx of multinational and European companies, and state controlled industries in search of cheap labour and subsidies has made the "rulers" even more invisible and gave a new quality to the Welsh/ruling England antagonism.

The core of the Welsh communities consisted of manual workers and their families, while the managers, supervisors and officials were frequently non-Welsh. Although the Welsh/ruling England antagonism had obscured the social differentiation of the Welsh community, the distance between the majority of working class people and the small group of Welsh professional people was substantial and had important political and cultural consequences. The nonconformist chapels strongly affected the relationships between the different occupational groups within the Welsh community. While the professional people accepted the values and norms of the chapel more thoroughly and consistently, the working class people had to achieve a compromise between the practical demands of daily life and older traditions, and the values and norms of the chapel. Welsh quarrymen also expressed their resentment against the chapels, for the chapels were used by the employers to control the workers and thereby helped to exploit them — membership of the hirer's chapel was often a condition for employment. Emmett argued that the different response to the norms and values of the chapel set limits to the relationship between leaders (professional people) and the led.

Even though she rejected Jenkins' *buchedd* system on the grounds that there was no division between rough pub people (*pobl y dafarn*) and cultured chapel people (*pobl y capel*), the interrelation of chapel and social structure in Blaenau showed a similar differentiation between the two groups according to observance of the chapel norms. It also showed that occupational status and religious status were closely related. However, the internal division of the Welsh community was muted because political and economic power were seen as the domain of ruling England. The life-styles — behaviour, appearance and language — of white-collar workers, shopkeepers, farmers and local businessmen were not visibly distinct from the working class life-style. For those who were comparatively wealthy, adopting a different life style would distance them socially from the community's traditional culture. "To do so would entail a loss of sociable contact, and of esteem which could hardly be compensated for by rewards from any claim to English status ..." (Emmett 1982a:184). Class opposition was merged into and strengthened by nationalist feelings which, in turn, united the community. Nevertheless, differences in wealth and status determined much of what happened in the community and were implicit in the conflicts within the community.

Although the increasing social differentiation since the Second World War had been expected to weaken the Welsh community/ruling England dichotomy, the contrary was the case. The growth of educational institutions, the civil service, the reorganization of local government (which made more senior posts available to Welshmen), the expansion of the media (radio and television), etc., led to an increase in the number of Welsh professional and technical workers — mainly in the centres of this development, Bangor and Caernarfon, where they were sufficiently numerous to form their own social groups which were characterized by a middle class life-style.

Emmett criticized Khleif's assumption that the new post-war Welsh middle class created a new sense of Welsh identity which she called "aggressive Welshness". She argued that the new "aggressive Welshness" emerged with the youth rebellion of the mid-1960s which she described in her article on "Blaenau Boys in the mid-1960s" published in 1978 (Emmett 1978). Her main concern was to show how the Blaenau youth resisted the temptation of Anglicization and transformed the meaning of Welshness. Emmett wanted to know how the youth rebellion of the mid-1960s had been initiated and by which forces it had been influenced. In 1976 she interviewed Blaenau men in their mid-twenties to explore the shared memory of their leisure activities during the mid-1960s. All men that she interviewed came from a Welsh working class background, they were raised with chapel values, went to Sunday School, spoke Welsh and inherited Welsh traditions. Emmett described them as influenced by "the quarrymen's tradition". Many of the teenagers in the mid-1960s had left a school which had offered them little to face the poor opportunities of an economically declining community.

During the 1960s the increasing division between the generations manifested itself in the rebellion of young people in most of the Western industrialized nations. Young people sought ways to distinguish themselves from the adults and started to question conventional beliefs. Emmett described it as a successful fight to win recognition of their right to more independence, which fought against the widespread belief that conformity to the existing values was in itself a virtue. The success of the youth movement had far-reaching consequences for society and the Blaenau boys of the mid-1960s were a part of this movement.

Although Blaenau was to a certain degree an isolated community surrounded by mountains, the young people came into contact with the developing youth sub-culture through radio, records, television, trips to English cities, visits by young people from English cities (mostly children of Blaenau emigrants) and by observation of the life style of the English middle class drop-outs who settled in the community. Three distinctive groups grew out of those young people who adopted "anti-establishment values": the mods, which were later called skinheads, the rockers or Hell's Angels, and the hippies. The boys who formed these groups all knew each other. Emmett believed that a smaller proportion of the Blaenau youth, than of the young people who lived in big cities, remained "square" because within a small face-to-face community everyone's behaviour was part of a public performance. Once the new styles were visible all young people were more or less touched by them.

In the 1950s and early 1960s the future of the Welsh language and culture looked dim. The bleak prospects of high unemployment, the economic pressure on the youth to speak English and leave Wales, the decline of the chapels and the estrangement of Plaid Cymru — which Emmett (1978:98) has described as "the property of intellectuals and returned exiles" — from the Welsh working class culture contributed to the crisis of Welsh identity. Under such circumstances the young people could have opted for Anglicization, however, they did the contrary. The ideas which were taken from outside the community were adapted to the life in a Welsh context and Anglicization was consciously rejected by all except one group — this group became only temporarily Anglicized. Although they rebelled against their parents, they were still accepted as part of the community which supported them in their Welshness. They developed a new consciously positive Welsh identity which also contributed to a more positive perception of Blaenau as a *Welsh* working class community, and a more open and direct expression of anti-English feelings by the ordinary Welsh people.

This more positive and self-conscious perception of community was important for Blaenau's development, for the powerful bodies in North Wales perceived the town as a "irremediably ugly", "backward" and dying community which would inevitably continue to decline (Emmett 1982a: 185). She complained that while smaller towns in Gwynedd — Porthmadog, Harlech, Bala and Dolgellau — had government offices and amenities, such as cinemas, public swimming pools, theatres, etc., Blaenau had none. That the Blaenau people were the "... largest and most disadvantaged of all these towns ..." (Emmett 1982a:188) was also evident in the local authorities' plans for economic development. In his recommendations for growth centres in Gwynedd the Welsh Council ignored Blaenau. The Gwynedd County Council followed this recommendation and the decision was reversed only after protests from Blaenau. Emmett believed that the basic problem of Blaenau was its lack of amenities. Although the Development Board for Rural Wales (DBRW) spent over £ 300,000 on the new joint Ffestiniog Railway and British Rail station which would bring increasing numbers of tourists to Blaenau, the lack of amenities would prevent them from staying in the town. As a result, the economic benefit for the community would be very limited[46]. The County Council and the DBRW also invested in training facilities and gave grants to the community centre and several clubs.

The revitalization of the community, Emmett assumed, was also encouraged by the nationalist movement. The reassertion of community could be seen as a response to the threat of the community by the increasing number of non-Welsh incomers. These incomers consisted mainly of two groups: manual workers who moved into the community to work on the major construction schemes (power stations), and urban refugees who came to Blaenau to try alternative life styles. Both groups are only accepted at the margins of the community and excluded from the mainstream of Welsh community life. For the consciously Welsh people the non-Welsh, especially the English, are a constant reminder — they are "representatives in the flesh" (Emmett 1982b:215) — of what they are opposed to. The Welsh/English conflict has further deepened because the attraction of cheap housing — the result of emigration — brought a great number of English into the area. More and more houses were bought by English people as second homes and subsequently the prices went up. This caused much resentment, for the local population could not afford to pay the high prices. In addition, it was feared that more English children in the schools, more English conversation in pubs, shops and at meetings would threaten the Welsh language[47]. However, Emmett (1982b:216) stated that those

---

46 The Blaenau Ffestiniog area was included in the 1989 draft of the Gwynedd Structure Plan as an area "within which, by reason of location, accessibility, natural resources, infrastructure and the capacity of the local community to absorb growth could provide suitable opportunities for development." (Cyngor Sir Gwynedd 1989, Policy Y1, p. 30)

English who did not conform too closely to the stereotype — pushy and lacking in understanding — "... receive from Welsh individuals friendship, indifference and enmity in roughly the same proportions as anyone else, within the limits set by their exclusion from the mainstream of the Welsh community's life." She also believed that the incomers, especially hippies and artists, have, by their positive view of Blaenau, contributed to the renewed pride Blaenau people have in their town.

The most important aspects in the study of Welsh rural communities were the problem of the survival of the Welsh language and culture — the Welsh/English antagonism — and the question as to whether a distinctive Welsh stratification system existed in the communities studied. Both groups, the native anthropologists of the Aberystwyth School and the English anthropologists, have placed an emphasis on these two aspects of social life in Welsh communities, however, their approaches differed markedly. Whereas the Welsh anthropologists were part of the largely middle class nationalist discourse of Welsh identity, which was aimed at creating a discrete *Welsh* middle class by constructing a suitable version of a distinctive Welsh culture, the English anthropologists followed different lines. Both Emmett and Frankenberg have been accused of ethnocentrism by Welsh scholars. Frankenberg (1990:176) gives an impression of the reaction of the Welsh intelligentsia to his study: "Welsh critics [...] argued that I not only failed to recognize difference but [...] was too ignorant, stupid and colonialist English even to perceive it." In a polemical comment on community studies in Wales, Glyn Williams (1980:169) accused Frankenberg (1957) and Emmett (1964) of perpetuating the ethnocentric *complex English civilization/primitive Welsh society* dichotomy by adopting an evolutionary perspective in their analysis of Welsh culture. He believed, that they envisaged the inevitable substitution of Welsh culture by English

---

47 The arson campaign of the secret Welsh nationalist organization *Meibion Glyndwr* was a consequence of this development. *Meibion Glyndwr* (Sons of Glyndwr) is a secret militant nationalist organization which fights for an independent Wales, for the maintenance of Welsh langauge and culture, and against the threats from "imperialist" English influence. It is responsible for the fire-bombing campaign against English holiday homes, etc. in recent years. Owain Glyndwr, from whom the organiztion derived its name, fought against the English conquerors (AD 1399-1410) and established a short lived independent Welsh nation; and Gwyn A. Williams (1991:87-113) believes that "... the Welsh mind is still haunted by its lightning-flash vision of a people that was free."

culture, as a result of the process of modernization, and concluded: "The impression is given that Welsh rural society is a somewhat endangered, primitive form of social organization which must yield to the larger, more complex forms of British society. The Welsh are placed in Nature, where basic instincts are given rein; whereas the English are the source of a civilisation which diffuses slowly to encompass Welsh society and culture."

Although Williams' criticism was certainly a bit too polemical, the studies of Frankenberg and Emmett were certainly biased. However, Frankenberg's and Emmett's approaches to the study of Welsh culture were to a large extent different. While Frankenberg adopted a Marxist perspective, which suffered from a preoccupation with structural aspects, Emmett's approach was either structural-functionalistic (Llanfrothen) or simply impressionistic (Blaenau Ffestiniog). Both authors suffered from the exclusion from the "mainstream of the Welsh community's life" and, therefore, their descriptions had to remain partial. Frankenberg's study of Glyn Ceiriog also suffered from his preoccupation with the function of institutions and the processes of conflict and cohesion, so important for his concept of the moving equilibrium; it showed little of the community's social life. I agree with Trefor M. Owen (1986:116), who said about Frankenberg: "His main interest was in the social processes stripped of their cultural idiom and reduced to functional terms." Frankenberg's study may be an interesting account of village politics, but it has done little to illuminate the complex processes of cultural change in the social life of a Welsh community under massive pressure from outside.

A recent sociological study of the Upper Ithon Valley, between Llandrindod Wells and Y Drenewydd (Newtown), in eastern mid-Wales by Graham Day, Jonathan Murdoch and the Institute of Earth Studies at Aberystwyth (Day & Murdoch 1993), is also preoccupied with institutional processes. The setting was chosen for its economic peripherality (little overt economic change was noticeable), however, in other spheres the changes were quite dramatic and resulted in a constant renegotiation of the conceptions of community, localness and belonging. Day and Murdoch (1993:108) argue that the notion of community is central to the processes of constructing the community's boundary. They focus on the roles of "incomers" and "locals" in the process. However, in contrast to Glyn Ceiriog (Frankenberg 1957; see pages 119-124), outsiders do not play an important role in village organizations. Strangers are denied access to key positions in local organizations which are run by members of long-established families. Day and Murdoch (1993:105) believe that the struggle to "represent" the community both politically and culturally and the struggle for the control of the key institutions will intensify with increasing inward migration to the valley. I have already explained in chapter 6 (see pages 58-59) that the conclusions from the analysis have to be viewed in a critical light because the qualitative data obtained were limited to so-called "key informants", which were thus defined because of their active participation in formal village organizations.

The area has a distinct Welsh identity although neither the Welsh language nor the "institutions that usually accompany it" (Day & Murdoch 1993:94) play an important role in the conceptualization of its Welshness — unfortunately, Day and Murdoch do not describe the factors which are important for the conceptualization of Welshness in the area. The cultural and social pressures which affect the community pose a threat to the maintenance of the distinctively Welsh rural way of life in this part of Wales.

The dominant economic institution is the family farm. It leads to a certain stability, however, the economic activities in the area as a whole are insufficiently linked to make a local economic system (in Margaret Stacey's (1974) sense). The boundaries of the agricultural system are ill defined because individual farmers have varied relationships with different economic markets; they are tied to national and international markets and depend on EC and state support. However, the long-established local farm families form a highly integrated social network which plays a key role in maintaining the structure of social relations in the area. The reproduction of the farm and the family are closely intertwined because economic actors are provided by the family with both motivation and resources (Day & Murdoch 1993:94-96). "Farming therefore constitutes very definitely a core economic activity, generating a range of shared experiences and interests within much of the local population." (Day & Murdoch 1993:96) Despite the processes of specialization and intensification, which led to growth in farm size at the expense of smaller farms who had less capital available to them, transformed versions of the old patterns of co-operation (cf. Rees; see page 91) survived. There is strong support for the idea of using local contractors as this creates employment in the valley. The use of local contractors is an important factor in the economy of area because outside farming the range of employment opportunities is narrow.

Day and Murdoch argue that the people have a strong sense of belonging to a particular place and that the involvement in various organizations provided links between the different communities in the valley as well as integrated the population of the area. The most important common theme in the valley was the extent to which local distinctiveness was under threat. "Many pressures were regarded as conspiring to undermine local identity, which was already somewhat fragile; as one informant commented:

English people tend to regard this area as Welsh; Welsh people regard it as English; it is caught in the middle, but has its own sense of identity. However, the place is losing its uniqueness, the transient population is increasing." (Day & Murdoch 1993:101-102)

Inward migration is regarded as a threat to local as well as cultural distinctiveness in many parts of Wales and the inward population movement is a process which is almost totally beyond local control. It is the result of economic forces of national housing market (high prices in the south of England, considerably lower prices in Wales) and the English tendency to idealize rural life — which was so pointedly described by Howard Newby (1979). For the local people, the changing housing situation — made worse by the constraints of environment protection and the lack of financial resources for new public authority housing, which are due to central government policies — was as significant as the changing employment opportunities. Apart from housing and inward migration, the most important influences derive from central state intervention. Farmers depend on state and EC grants and subsidies. Employment opportunities are subject to the employment creating and concentrating activities of rural development agencies. The supply of services for the communities in the valley has suffered from the state's drive for centralization and "cost-effectiveness".

Interaction between members of long established, well-integrated households and newcomers was a major factor in stimulating a discussion of what it means to belong. Day and Murdoch (1993:108) argue that "incomers" and "locals" recognize that they have to live together in a confined physical and social space and that this compels them to interact and negotiate the notion of community. Locals do not want strangers and their midst and newcomers do not want to remain strangers, and, Day and Murdoch say, some effort was made to incorporate newcomers in village organizations. "In the process of negotiation, the identities of individual participants and of the places to which they belong change. Different places remain distinctive, according to the patterns of resolution reached between old and new residents." (Day & Murdoch 1993:108) Unfortunately, Day and Murdoch do not show in what way the concept of the community changes. The incomers and the long-established locals may present two totally different public faces of the community boundary because local symbols are invested with different meanings by members of the different groups. There appears to be little consensus about what is threatened, although both groups may agree that the community is threatened by outside forces. In the case of newcomers this seems to be paradoxical because the newcomers themselves, with their idealized notion of rural community life, are part of the outside forces which threaten the community. Incomers will certainly change the nature of the rural community, but Days and Murdoch's account does not further our understanding of how the complex process of living and interacting of locals and newcomers will influence, and perhaps totally transform, the community boundary. Although Day and Murdoch (1993:103) mention that relations are not always smooth, the potential for conflicts between locals and newcomers seems to be underestimated — this may be due to their field research methods (see pages 58-59). The situation described by Howard Newby (1979:167) for English rural communities, that resentment among the local population grows when the pressure of the newcomers on the housing market makes it impossible for young local families to find a house, is certainly also true for Wales. In the Welsh-speaking areas of north Wales the housing problem, or the English immigration problem, is also inextricably connected with the perceived threat to the Welsh language and culture. Resentment is high and finds a militant expression in the firebombing campaigns by Meibion Glyndwr. Even in the Upper Ithon valley, a comparatively Anglized area, there is a serious feeling of injustice which is expressed in ethnic terms (Welsh vs. English). "One farmer voiced very strong feelings about 'English people coming in and altering our way of life locally. I don't mind home building as long as it's not for outsiders. We need the homes for the young and elderly; but English people are comming in and taking over the area'." (Day & Murdoch 1993:106-107)

The development of nationalist sentiments is often assumed to be the reaction to the threat to Welsh culture (cf. Khleif 1980; Emmett 1982a, 1982b; Day & Suggett 1985). For Emmett (1982a:167) it "... is simply the case that the consciousness of national identity saturates life ..." in North Wales. However, such *as a matter of fact* statements are far too simple and contribute only to the maintenance of the nationalist mythology. A more productive approach was adopted by Day and Suggett (1985). 'Nation', they said, can be regarded as a variant of 'community' on a different level because ideas of belonging, of identity and of the communal are an integral part of nationalist concepts. Nationalism as an ideological construct, as Anthony Smith (1991:91) has argued, seeks to inspire a spirit of national solidarity between its members by seeing the nation "as a family writ large" — in the case of Welsh nationalism, *as a small rural community writ large*, it, thus, postulates the social unity of the nation. Day and Suggett suggested that it was time to deconstruct the nationalist ideas, myths and definitions. Nationalism should be seen as a phenomenon of political practice and ideological discourse. "This means that we need to treat 'Wales' as it has figured in successive, and rival, discourses, and consider the question 'How many Wales?' or 'How many ways of being Welsh?' " (Day & Suggett 1985:96)

In contrast to Emmett, Day and Suggett, who also believed that nationality was part of everyday consciousness in Wales, distinguished between situational use of ethnicity at the "immediate level of daily life" and the situational use of nationality which operated on the political level. Emmett had failed to do so, and subsequently confused the consciousness of Welsh ethnic identity rooted in the individual's experience of himself within the collectivity (the community), that indeed saturates life in North Wales, with the largely political/ideological concept of a national identity. However, the nationalist discourse has certainly contributed to the heightened awareness the Welsh people have of their own ethnic identities. I use the plural, *ethnic identities*, to emphasize that there is no single concept of Welsh identity. This also implies the crucial difference of national identity and ethnic identities in the Welsh context. Nationalist ideologies are constructed to gain or secure the hegemony of a specific section of society and serve to form social alliances containing a variety of different elements and sections of society (Day & Suggett 1985:98), under the leadership of the section dominating the contents of the discourse. The hegemony, as Day and Suggett have pointed out, is the process in which the relations between leaders and led are reproduced through an organization of consent. Although this process involves conflict between the leaders and the followers which results in a constantly changing ideology, its main objective, the formation of a unifying national identity through the reconciliation and re-interpretation of the different meanings of Welsh identity, is not subject to this change. I agree with Day and Suggett on the point that a concept of nationalism which constructs it as a rigid block of ideas corresponding to a given social class, or ethnic collectivity has to be rejected, and that: "Nationalism provides one of the (continually present?) ideological forms through which men and women may become conscious of, or try to make sense of, their social existence as it is transformed over time." (Day & Suggett 1985:98)

However, I would argue that the preoccupation with nationalism and national identity has led to an underestimation of the significance of the complex conceptualizations of Welsh identities at the community level. The antagonism which is omnipresent in the consciousness of Welsh people — Emmett has quite rightly called it the *Welsh community*/ruling England antagonism (unfortunately she did not continue along this line but turned to national identity instead) — is not primarily conceptualized in terms of Wales as a nation versus ruling England, rather the most significant concept is that of WE as a particular Welsh community versus THEM as ruling England.

In a recent article John Borland, Ralph Fevre and David Denney (Borland et al. 1992) have shown the centrality of the concept of community to various variants of Welsh nationalist ideology. They have analyzed the social constructions of community and their relationships to variants of nationalist ideology, which exist simultaneously within the same social space. The objective of their research was to develop an explanation for the upsurge in nationalist activity in North West Wales in the 1980s. They quite rightly argue that an analysis of Plaid Cymru's and Meibion Glyndwr's success in terms of Thatcherism misconstrues the nature of Welsh nationalism which is based on the conviction that *Y Fro Gymraeg* (the Welsh heartland) is the last bastion of a unique culture different to the rest of the UK. Unfortunately, their analysis of the mobilization of political support for nationalist groups is based on rather weak theoretical foundations. Community, they argue, is the most important concept in the process of political mobilization. However, their discussion of community as a social construction which is constructed at its boundaries simply ignores the anthropological approaches to the symbolic construction of community which have been discussed in the previous chapter, and, as a result, they attempt to put the cart before the horse. As Cohen has pointed out in 1982, the higher the societal level of collective representation, the more simplified is the collective representation — resulting in a rather crude reflection of the character of its constituents. "*Local experience mediates national identity,* and, therefore, an anthroplogical understanding of the latter cannot proceed without knowledge of the former." (Cohen 1982b:13)

A lecture by Raymond Williams to a Plaid Cymru Summer School in 1977 is presented by Borland, Fevre and Denney as the best illustration of the social construction of community in the Welsh context. Williams stressed the social obligation which grew out of the sense of being of the locality and the sense of common identity which it provided. The notion of obligation is taken up by them to construct a relationship between material support and the "imagined" nature of the community (a concept borrowed from Anderson 1983). They argue (Borland et al. 1992:53) that people belonging to a place have a notion of obligation which in turn produces "*tangible material* gains; thus the *imagined* or *socially constructed* appears to become *concrete.*"

Their approach suffers from a rather superficial "materialist" perception of the concrete. It is not the aspect of material gains which makes the construction of community concrete. As anthropological studies of communities in Britain have shown, it is the experience of, similarity and difference, and the emotional attachment to a place and its people, which is a concrete psychological experience for the individual. The notion of obligation arises form the feeling of belonging and, in turn, the fulfulment of obligations reinforces the feeling. In the process of thinking oneself into difference, the process of symbolically constructing the boundaries of the community, the community is thought into being. Constructions of the mind are no less concrete than material gains.

Two further aspects of Williams' description of the social construction of community, the habit of mutual obligation and the influence of outside forces, are discussed. Both are supposed to add significantly to the concretization of the imagining of community. The habit of mutual obligation is said to be a mechanism of social control which by binding individuals together can result in individual gain or expose individuals to exploitation. Based on this, is the production of an image of the "good society" — which invokes a Tönnies' style *Gemeinschaft* — where exploitation and conflicts of interest do not exist, and the good of the individual will be the common good and vice versa. Secondly, the social construction of community is affected by forces which are seen as being outside the community. Here, the community/society dichotomy is resurrected: community is imagined as affirmed by direct knowledge and experience, society, on the other hand, is seen as distant and dehumanized, unknown and not experienced. The interaction with the outside world, which is crucial for the construction of the community boundary, is reduced to the interaction with the distant urban society of nationalist ideology. Forces affecting the community can also originate in a neighbouring community, in a similar cultural context.

For their analysis of four variants of nationalist ideology in relationship to different constructions of community they developed six questions from their rather superficial theoretical discussion. The central question is (1) "who seems to be of the place?" Related to the central question are five more questions concerning, (2) the substance of social obligation, (3) the basis of common identity, (4) the forms of collective struggle, (5) the view of the "good society" (*Gemeinschaft*), (6) and the way in which society (*Gesellschaft* or the "bad society") is seen to be threatening the community (cf. Borland et al. 1992:55). It cannot surprise that all four variants of nationalist ideology — the "open community", the two variants of the "culturally closed community" (based on a religious and a secular construction), and the "racially closed community", stress the threat for the community by outside, English, forces. However, the concepts differ significantly in regard to the other questions. The ability to locate oneself in a particular place and the basis of common identity are two aspects of belonging which are inseparably connected — Borland, Fevre and Denney's stress of locality appears to be too simplistic and rather misleading. A sense of place is crucial for the individuals feeling of belonging and also creates a common identity among individuals who are of the same place and vice versa.

The "modernist" variant of nationalist ideology, the "Open Community", is advocated by the so-called modernist faction of Plaid Cymru led by the president Dafydd Elis-Thomas. According to the modernists all people living and working in Wales who share the beliefs in peace, ecology, etc., and would fight against threats to their local community (including Welsh langauge and culture) belong to a local Welsh community and, thus, to the Welsh nation, which is envisaged as a community of communities.

Cymdeithas yr Iaith Gymraeg (Welsh Language Society) stands for a variant of nationalist ideology which is based on the culturally closed community[48] and where the ability to speak Welsh defines who belongs to the commu-

---

48 Another variant of the culturally closed community is the one based on religious values (Borland et al. 1992:60-62). However, this category is based almost entirely on a single radio interview with the theologist Prof. Tudur Jones. It has been omitted

nity. "The community exists to maintain the language, the language exists to give identity to individuals, and to sustain the community and the nation." (Borland et al. 1992:63). The notion of the racially closed community, in which the Welsh language also plays a central part, adds a metaphysical component to the concept of community. It is advocated by the militant nationalists of *Meibion Glyndwr* (Sons of Glyndwr) and *Adfer* (Restore). At the centre of the construction lies the concept of the spirit of Welshness, *eneidfaeth*. *Eneidfaeth* is a mystical entity, supposed to be a product of the ancestors, that creates man's personality. It lies at the heart of the Welsh community and only those born in the countryside can have it (can be Welsh). The spirit is inextricably connected with the land and, therefore, even those Welsh people born in a Welsh community who live outside Wales are excluded from the spiritual community (Borland et al. 1992:64-66).

Borland, Fevre and Denney (Borland et al. 1992:66) argue that community in north-west Wales operates as a "site of resistance" and a social mechanism which binds individuals together. "It contains a set of ideas that simultaneously define what is and what should be, it forms a context of social organization and acts as a defence against pressures of external economic exploitation." The social construction of community has important social and economic effects. People who belong to the community can claim a greater right to the goods of the community (jobs, houses, education).

That the concept of community is central to all variants of Welsh nationalist ideologies comes as no surprise. However, Borland, Fevre and Denney fail to understand the diversity of meanings which make up the substance of community from the inside by devoting their attention to nationalist representations of community. In this sense, the paper does not provide the support for the revival of community in sociology that the authors claim. It is certainly an interesting, although theoretically superficial, contribution to the understanding of a specific mode of representation of community in nationalist discourse. It tells us very little of the private face of a Welsh communities boundary, which would enable us to understand why the concept of "community" has such a salience in the discourse of Welsh nationalism.

---

because the religious based construction appears to be of very limited influence in contemporary Wales.

CONCLUSION

AN "ALMOST TRIBAL THING": COMMUNITY AND IDENTITY IN NORTH WALES

Glyn Williams (1980:169) has criticized the picture of Welsh society presented in the anthropological studies of rural community in Wales as a "loosely defined Welsh way of life". Anthropologists wrote extensively about structural aspects of Welsh society, religion, the Welsh community/ ruling England antagonism, etc., and little about the meaning Welsh identity and the Welsh community had for its members in the early and late 1950s. I would argue that the community study approach which is concerned with the members' perceptions of their community and the complex processes of how they manage to create and maintain its boundary through the use of symbolism is particularly relevant for the study of Welsh communities and ethnic identities in a rapidly changing society. This is especially relevant because the economic and social changes which have influenced the development of Welsh society since the 1950s led to a decline of many distinctive structural features, such as the status system created by the nonconformist chapels, or the lack of an influential Welsh-speaking Welsh bourgeoisie.

Kenneth O. Morgan (1971:171) has called Welsh cultural nationalism "... a crusade not only against the dominance of English but even against the twentieth century itself, and the inexorable encroachments of an alien, Anglo-Saxon world." As we have seen, Welsh cultural nationalism, with its emphasis on the small, isolated rural community, its search for roots in a medieval Welsh society, its anti-urbanism, its emphasis on the alienating effects of industrial society, has much in common with Tönnies' ideas about the *Gemeinschaft/Gesellschaft* dichotomy. However, there is one crucial difference between the two concepts. While Tönnies attributed the negative effects of change to the largely anonymous forces of capitalism, the ideologues of Welsh cultural nationalism were able to couch their critique of modernization in terms of a historical experience, more immediate to the ordinary Welsh people: the experience of *ruling England*. However, the fact that this experience is shared by all Welsh people, whether they speak Welsh or not, is often obliterated, or even consciously negated, by postulating that without the Welsh language there would be no distinctive Welsh identity. In a study of six rural communities in Mid-Wales[49] G. Clare Wenger (1980:120-122) has shown that the salience of Welsh national identity appears to be correlated with Welsh-speaking rather than Welsh ethnic identity. She argued that Welsh ethnic identity seems to become more salient when local values are threatened by outsiders. Thus, concepts such as the Welsh community/ruling England dichotomy are used by all groups of Welsh people, Welsh-speaking and non-Welsh-speaking, to express resistance to those changes imposed from outside which are believed to be a threat to the community. The Welsh historian Glanmor Williams (1979:32-33) has warned that the emphasis on the language as the core of Welsh ethnic identity might lead to a division of Wales into two parts coexisting in mutual incomprehension. He called for the recognition and reconciliation of the different identities of Welsh-speaking and non-Welsh-speaking Welsh because many factors besides the language which were part of the process of creating a sense of Welsh identity are shared by all Welsh regardless of their language. He urged the Welsh-speaking people to recognize that the non-Welsh-speaking Welsh have a right to their Welsh identity, and the non-Welsh-speaking people to understand the deep concerns the Welsh-speaking Welsh have for the survival of the language and the culture of Wales.

He wrote: "What is called for from the non-Welsh-speaking majority, especially, is a positive act of imaginative sympathy to try to understand the near-desperation of the minority at the dire prospects for the language and the culture based on it. The Welsh-speaking minority need to recognize more readily than some of them always do that there are a great many of their countrymen who find deeply hurtful the suggestion that those who do not speak the Welsh language are to be regarded as being either not Welsh at all or at best second-class Welsh people." (Glanmor Williams 1979:33)

Thus, the research into Welsh ethnic identity cannot be confined to *Y Fro Gymraeg*, the Welsh heartland. To gain insights into the conceptualization of Welsh ethnic identity, as well as national identity, we have to

---

[49] Bala, Abermaw (Barmouth), Rhayader, Tregaron and Caron-Is-Clawdd parish, Corris and Talylln parish and the parishes of Llanllugan and Llanwyddelan.

deconstruct the nationalist myths that non-Welsh-speaking Welsh have no Welsh identity and that the ethnic identity of the Welsh-speaking Welsh is monolithic.

An important aspect of the confusion of Welsh national identity with ethnic identity is inherent in the approaches to the study of community which place their emphasis on structure rather than meaning, for they can only reveal the public face (see page 49) of the community. The equation of Welsh national identity with ethnic identity leads to the fallacy of taking the public face — the common mask created by a unifying ideology — of the community as the real community. However, the public face is only a stereotype behind which the internal variety disappears, in the case of a predominantly Welsh-speaking rural community this means that the internal contradictions and conflicts, the results of the different meanings attached to Welsh identity by different segments of the community, will not be recognized.

The community studies in Wales have shown that the anthropologists were either, in case of the Aberystwyth School and Emmett, preoccupied with the culturally distinctive structural forms of Welsh society, or, in the case of Frankenberg, with the structural forms of institutions, whose meaning was taken for granted because they could be found throughout Britain. The problems that these studies have ignored, or even obscured, were the interrelated problems of the conceptualization and maintenance of ethnic and community boundaries.

The communities studied were all subject to intensive social change which made a purely structural-functional approach particularly problematic. The loss of isolation of the rural communities through the mass media and the influx of English people, the increasing self-consciousness of the new Welsh middle class, bilingual language policies and the increasing importance of Welsh language education, the increasing tendency to reserve a large proportion of the labour market to Welsh-speakers by making proficiency in Welsh a precondition for employment, the widened gap between the developed regions of southern England and the underdeveloped regions of Wales, the devastating effects of the *take-it-from-the-poor-give-it-to-the-rich* policies, such as the Poll Tax, of the Conservative governments have all contributed to the changing face of Welsh society. However, as a result of the structural-functionalist accounts in the past and the lack of recent *anthropological* studies of Welsh communities we have a static picture of the Welsh community. The relevance of research into the impact of modernization on local communities has been demonstrated by A. P. Cohen. He has argued that, as a result of social change imposed upon the community from outside, the structural boundaries of the community may be replaced by symbolically constituted boundaries. Furthermore, the fact that structural forms were imported does not mean that their meaning was transferred unchanged and imposed upon the members of the community. The young people of Blaenau described by Emmett have shown that the imported forms became media for the reassertion and symbolic expression of the Welsh community's boundary through their transformation into an idiom more consonant with indigenous culture — the idiom of the Welsh/ruling England antagonism as expressed in local Welsh identity. Thus, the forms of rebellion against the establishment, which were developed outside the community, led to a reassertion of Welsh identity firmly rooted in communal identity.

The important role of the community for the creation and maintenance of ethnic identity in Wales, supports Cohen's hypothesis that the community could be the most adequate medium for the collective expression of each member's whole self. The community is a reality that hinges crucially on the consciousness of its members because the social process of everyday life within the community contains all the sentiments attached to kinship and neighbourhood, friendship and familiarity. This is evident in the perception of the Welsh community by a Welsh-speaking informant who saw the "Welsh mind" in contrast to the "colonial mind" of the English who see Wales as a colony where they can treat the natives as they like.

> *The Welsh mind has always been like that — like a small island mentality. A limited scope, ah — limited thinking — community mind, and that's it.*

Cohen (1982b:5-6) argued that the feeling of belonging is evoked by the shared knowledge of the ins-and-outs of everyday life, by the knowledge of the way of doing things. This is reflected in the way the Welsh-speaking informants characterized their communities, e.g.:

> *I think any — because all the Welsh people are local to Blaenau, and we have only got a couple of English — All the locals know everybody, and know all the ins and outs of every relationship, every, you know. So the English person would maybe feel out because of the — he wouldn't know the* [ins and outs].

Furthermore, the Welsh/England antagonism is most immediate on the community level. It is here that the Welsh people directly experience the impact of the English incomers and of state bureaucracy — which is still perceived as ruling England, although it is increasingly Welsh at the local and county level. This is, first of all, perceived as a threat to the community and the assertion of Welsh ethnic identity is a means to strengthen its boundaries. The Welsh language is the most clear-cut criterion for the distinctiveness of a Welsh community, and it, therefore, stands at the forefront of the public face presented to the outside. In case of Blaenau Ffestiniog, Emmett has shown that the reassertion of Welsh identity led to a reassertion of community, which, in turn, contributed to the survival of the community as a basis for the production of Welsh identity. Thus, Welsh identity and communal identity are both part of a dialectical process which ensures the continuity of distinctiveness. The importance of community identity is evident in the rivalries between different communities which are fostered by stereotypes. For example, informants from Blaenau thought that the rivalry between different communities, Blaenau and Porthmadog, was stronger than the anti-English feeling:

It's a sort of — almost tribal thing — It is the easiest way I can think of it. When you're getting right down to basics. You're not as good as me, because you don't have got the same bit as me, see what I mean. You don't come from my little patch, my little area, so, therefore you're just not as good as me.

This rivalry which finds it regular, almost ritual, expression in fights between the men of both villages was confirmed by an informant who was born in Porthmadog:

Tribalism exists, yes, no doubt about that! One of the great Welsh passions and traditions is fights between villages. ... I do not like people from Blaenau. I don't know what it is about them but they're different. Ahm — if I see a person from Blaenau he reminds me of a sheep.
... And these quite often may be from respectable people, you know, totally normal and sane otherwise, but once it comes to a mention of Blaenau in Porth, you know, all rationality disappears, and it is a historical thing!

Hostilities between youth groups from neighbouring communities, described by Peters (1972, see pages 92-93) as a kind of symbolic enactment, a ritual of community, are still part of the repertoire of communal action:

> ... *last year, the beginning of last year [1988], up until summer, [...] there were fights between rival groupings from Porthmadog and Blaenau. Blaenau lads would go down and beat the blooming daylights out of the Porthmadog lads and then there would be a re-match set up somewhere, where Porthmadog lads would beat the blooming daylights out of the Blaenau lads.*
> *You find that by the time they're in the twenties they are usually settling down and getting married. They tend not to go out fighting quite as much. I don't say, they stop. They tend not to do quite as much.*

It is important to distinguish between what is called Welsh national identity, which is certainly based on and continuously informed by the sense of Welsh community identity, but which is to a great extent confined to the political expression of Welshness to the outside non-Welsh world. Political nationalism seems to be an increasingly relevant criterion for the internal differentiation of the Welsh community. Welsh-speaking people known to emphasize national identity are frequently labelled *Welsh nationalist* or *very Welsh* in contrast to the ordinary Welsh people who are simply *Welsh*. One Welsh-speaking informant expressed this as the contrast between the nationalists who believe Welsh identity to be superior to other identities and those who say: *being Welsh is ... 'be as you've always been'*. These *very Welsh* people, like the headmaster of a small primary school in Gwynedd, saw the ability to speak the language and the right to make decisions for the benefit of the Welsh people as essential for Welsh identity:

> *Welsh identity to me is being able to speak Welsh and being involved in decision making. Ah —, you know, that we can make decisions to benefit our own needs.*
> *... It's very hard to create a Welsh identity within our present government system. ... It's very difficult for an area like Gwynedd to provide an identity, and I think it's, you know, it's done that exceptionally well over the years. ... We are trying to create a Welsh identity within Europe. Now, I think that's easier than the other one* [creating a Welsh identity within Britain], *you know, and hopefully we will get backing from the European Parliament, to promote our identity as a nation.*

The promotion of the Welsh language is central to the nationalist cause and Glyn Williams (1986:188-189) has argued that the previously important domains of language reproduction, family, community and chapel have been eroded as a result of economic restructuring and the associated mobility of labour it has created. Increasing in-migration resulted in a substantial language group exogamy, which meant that the family was no longer able to reproduce the language to the extent that it once did. The community as a domain of language reproduction was also undermined by in-migration. Furthermore, secularization and the advent of the welfare state have undermined the chapel's reproductive role. As an answer to the decline of the Welsh language the Welsh language movement — most notably the *Cymdeithas yr Iaith Gymraeg* (Welsh Language Society) that was founded in 1962[50] — developed which tried to fight the effects of these changes by relegitimizing and reinstitutionalizing Welsh language reproduction in other domains, such as administration, education and the media. Colin H. Williams (1984:119-120) listed four reforms gained by the language movement. Firstly, the introduction of a nationwide bilingual education system from nursery to university level; secondly, the official use of bilingual forms and translators in administration and legislation; thirdly, the establishment of a Welsh-medium television channel, S4C (Sianel Pedwar Cymru); lastly, as the effect of these reforms a parallel system where Welsh and English are legitimized in administrative, legal, educational and entertainment spheres. Nevertheless, the reinstitutionalization of Welsh language reproduction in these domains made increased the dependency of the Welsh-speaking Welsh on state agencies for legitimization and financial support. Colin H. Williams (1984:121) argued that the reinstitutionalization of the Welsh language was likely to divide the Welsh working class, dependent on the declining traditional socio-economic context of Welsh-speaking communities, and the Welsh middle class, dependent on the institutions the language revival has created. Furthermore, a dramatic effect of this change was the emergence of an intra-Welsh class division along language lines. As a consequence of the change in the reproductional domains, Glyn Williams (1986:189) wrote, "... we begin to see the emergence of class varieties of Welsh — a feature which hitherto was absent. This in turn leads to a struggle within language, a struggle over language purity, a struggle with clear class dimensions."

---

50 A list of organizations which promoted the Welsh language can be found in Khleif 1980:63-73.

Excerpts from interviews from a Welsh-speaking middle class informant (teacher) and a Welsh-speaking working class informant (quarryman) illustrate the growing tensions and the class dimension of the struggle within the language in regard to the role of the Welsh language in the public sector. The teacher stressed the importance of the modernization of the Welsh language and argued for an unilingual Welsh education system:

> *And if the system can not cope with that, then you have to blame the system. Why should we, why should the Welsh language pander to the English hierarchy in that, or the English system in that sense. ... You know, I want the right to speak my own language — whenever — I want the right to use the public services and to be able to use Welsh, with the public services. I essentially want — I do not want to be treated as a second class citizen in my own country because I want to use my own language. And, in essence, I see this situation is quite simple. I will not get anything by being reasonable ... .*

A different attitude to the use of Welsh in the public sector was shown by the Welsh-speaking quarryman in a discussion of a bilingual leaflet concerning the privatization of the Welsh Water Authorities. The official Welsh used in these bilingual forms and leaflets is perceived as a mockery of Welsh-speaking intellectuals form South Wales:

> *When we get forms, bilingual, ya, I always go to the English one, you know. ... It took me — they made up words and they go back to South Wales, you know, South Wales. ... It's difficult reading. It's difficult, you know. You've got to think. If there is a word there, to break it up, you know, to find out what it means.... You wouldn't go round to your friends, speaking this kauder-Welsh. ... Terrible. This we've got to put up with, you see.*
> *... They're the kind of people doing it. Extremists! These are mocking words, you know, they are new, they're knew to me, anyway. I'm sure they make them up themselves, yeah. They got an English word there, you know that didn't sound Welsh, you know. And they break it up — .*

From the excerpt cited above it is evident that this has produced some kind of estrangement of the middle class from Welsh working class culture. It is interesting to note that the blame was not put on the middle class in general or the local Welsh authorities, but rather to extreme nationalists from

South Wales. That distance in the form of different language codes seems to be conceptualized in terms of cultural stereotypes, is probably due to the closeness of the Welsh community. People who have acquired middle class jobs are likely to come from working class families — since this new Welsh middle class is largely a post-1945 phenomenon (cf. Khleif 1984) — and bound to working class members of the community by kinship ties. Furthermore, the different language code is still confined to the written language, while the everyday Welsh is shared by members of all classes. Emmett found that the life-styles of the Welsh middle class were not visibly distinct from the working class life-style and that the internal divisions were masked by the Welsh/England dichotomy. In the case of the Welsh language they seem to be masked by the South Wales/North Wales dichotomy. In contrast to Gwynedd, where the majority of the population is Welsh-speaking, the southern parts of Wales are predominantly English-speaking (see Fig. 3). In addition to that different dialects of Welsh are spoken in North and South Wales.

An important factor for the maintenance of Welsh identity and community cohesion lies in the emphasis on egalitarianism within the Welsh community. The data from the area only a few miles from Llanfrothen seem to confirm Emmett's (1964:141) assumption, that the Welsh people took their strength from their sense of being working class people as opposed to the upper class people. Welsh identity seems to be conceived as inextricably connected with a sense of working class identity. Inside a Welsh community class distinctions seem not to be an important criterion for the categorization of the relationships between its members. Class categories are almost exclusively used to describe Welsh-English relations. One reason for this lies in the continuing cultural division of labour. Despite the rise of a new Welsh middle class, which holds positions previously reserved to Englishmen (in administration, etc.), a cultural division of labour still exists in most industries. Evidence for the persistence of a cultural division of labour can be found in the attitudes of the management towards their predominately Welsh work-force. The story told by a former employee of a large firm in North Wales provides a good example:

> *We used to have bosses coming over, you know, [...] they've been to Dubai somewhere, you know. And [...] when you hear this, how they treated the workers there. [...]. Ah — they come back to us, you know. And we had one*

or two of them. They were treating us, you know, like treating the blacks I think, you know.

While Emmett could not imagine how Welsh culture, with its emphasis on egalitarianism, could survive after the rise of a new middle class, the community seems to have found a way to maintain its unity. In this context it is very interesting to note how members of new Welsh-middle-class section within the Welsh community conceptualize Welsh identity.

In their study of "Politics of Rural Wales", P. J. Madgwick, Non Griffiths, and Valerie Walker (1973:145-146) described a certain reluctance of some middle class Welsh-speakers to identify themselves with the middle class. Emmett (1982a:184) described the pressures on the middle class people in Blaenau to conform to the working class life-style. Not to conform would mean the loss of sociable contact and status within the Welsh system which in a predominantly Welsh community could not be compensated for by a rise in the English status system. Those middle class informants which we interviewed in 1989 emphasized their working class background, probably, because to identify with the middle class would imply a loss of Welshness. Furthermore, the class system was seen as different to that of Britain as a whole, because the Welsh system was perceived as less rigid — offering more opportunities for working class people to rise in status.

> *But the — you know, the whole — it's very difficult to describe but they've definitely — in not the same — kind of class system. The language doesn't count, you know, there isn't — there isn't a cluster of two within the language, in that sense. Although — clearly, the better educated you are the better — the better speech you will have, in one sense, you know. I think that has — whether that education and class, you know, how much they go together. — Welsh improved — the Welsh have moved up the — moved up from, you can say, working class to middle class jobs. Not through — being born into it but by having to work to it and then education was the usual way of doing. So, it is not unusual to have — it is not unusual to have doctors, solicitors, and so on, from working class families. Much less — much more so — you know, it's much less unusual than it would be for working class families in England.*

In his study of Glyn Ceiriog, Frankenberg concluded: "Thus the village society in this stage of its history goes one, if not all, of the way towards uniting in a community of interest those who on the national level may be bitterly divided." (Frankenberg 1957:64)

However, the tensions which have arisen from the rise of a new Welsh middle class, the growing importance of the language movement and the nationalist movement since the 1950s will lead to further changes in the concept of Welsh identity. Much will depend on a reconciliation of the different meanings of Welsh identity, both within the Welsh-speaking population and between Welsh-speaking and the English-speaking Welsh people. In an article first published in 1965 and reprinted as a contribution to the devolution debate in 1978, Alwyn D. Rees (1978) argued that Wales was a nation with a split personality and urged his fellow Welshmen to face their Britishness. He argued that the Welsh should not push their "British complex" into the sub-consciousness, where it will only paralyse them, but face it and either overcome it or learn to live with it.

"In a situation in which, were we to be weighed and measured, we would all be found wanting, accusations in the spirit 'Welshier than thou' are of little use. Of no use, either, is the complementary condition, namely the feeling of guilt that impels us to attribute ulterior motives to those of different political persuasion who do for Wales as much as, if not more than, we ourselves. All these things are no more than the tricks and stratagems that allow us to escape from coming face to face with ourselves." (Rees 1978:13)

I believe that the discussion of the theoretical background of community studies, and the discussion of Welsh identity and community, class and nationalism has shown that social anthropological studies of Welsh communities concerned with the members' perception of their community and ethnic group can contribute much to an understanding of the complex and seemingly contradictory aspects of Welsh culture today.

BIBLIOGRAPHY

Official Papers ◀

CYNGOR SIR GWYNEDD (1989), *Cynllun Fframwaith Gwynedd—Memorandwm Esboniadol, Drafft,* Cynhyrchwyd gan Adran Gynllunio Cyngor Sir Gwynedd, Cyngor Sir Gwynedd, Caernarfon, Ionawr 1989.

[GWYNEDD COUNTY COUNCIL (1989), *Gwynedd Structure Plan—Explanatory Memorandum, Draft,* Produced by Gwynedd County Planning Department, Gwynedd County Council, Caernarfon, January 1989.]

Bibliography ◀

ANDERSON, BENEDICT (1983), *Imagined Communities: Reflections on the Origin and Spread of Nationalism,* Verso, London.

ARDENER, EDWIN (1987), 'Remote Areas': Some Theoretical Considerations, in: Anthony Jackson (ed.), *Anthropology at Home,* ASA Monograph 25, Tavistock, London and New York: 38 - 54.

ARENSBERG, CONRAD M. (1968), *The Irish Countryman - An Anthropological Study,* Natural History Press, Garden City [first published London 1937].

ARENSBERG, CONRAD M. & KIMBALL, SOLON T. (1968), *Family and Community in Ireland,* Harvard University Press, Cambridge, Mass [2nd and revised edn.].

ARENSBERG, CONRAD M. & KIMBALL, SOLON T. (1972), *Culture and Community,* Peter Smith, Gloucester, Mass.

ARENSBERG, CONRAD M. & KIMBALL, SOLON T. (1974), Community Studies: Retrospect and Prospect, in: Colin Bell & Howard Newby (eds.), *The Sociology of the Community: a Selection of Readings,* Frank Cass, London: 335 - 355.

AULL DAVIES, CHARLOTTE (1983), Welsh Nationalism and the British State, in: Glyn Williams (ed.), *Crisis of Economy and Ideology: Essays on Welsh Society,* S.S.R.C./ B.S.A. Sociology of Wales Study Group, Bangor: 201 - 213.

BARNES, J. A. (1969), Class and Committees in Norwegian Island Parish, in: Robert Mills French (ed.), *The Community — A Comparative Perspective*, Peacock Publishers, Itasca: 122 - 139 [first published in Human Relations VII (1), 1954].

BARTH, FREDRIK (1969), Introduction, in Fredrik Barth (ed.), *Ethnic Groups and Boundaries — The Social Organization of Culture Difference*, Universitets Forlaget, Bergen - Oslo, George Allen & Unwin, London: 9 - 38.

BELL, COLIN & NEWBY, HOWARD (1971), *Community Studies — An Introduction to the Sociology of the Local Community*, George Allen & Unwin, London.

BELL, COLIN & NEWBY, HOWARD & ROSE, DAVID & SAUNDERS, PETER (1978), Rural Community and Rural Community Power, in: Howard Newby (ed.), *International Perspectives on Rural Sociology*, John Wiley & Sons, Chichester: 55 - 85.

BLOCH, MAURICE (1985), *Marxism and Anthropology*, Oxford University Press, Oxford.

BOISSEVAIN, JEREMY (1975), Introduction: Towards a Social Anthropology of Europe, in: Jeremy Boissevain & John Friedl (eds.), *Beyond the Community: Social Process in Europe*, Dept. of Educational Science of the Netherlands, the Hague: 9 - 17.

BOON, JAMES A. (1982), *Other Tribes, Other Scribes — Symbolic Anthropology in the Comparative Study of Culture, Histories, Religions, and Texts*, Cambridge University Press, Cambridge.

BORLAND, JOHN & FEVRE, RALPH & DENNEY, DAVID (1992), Nationalism and Community in North West Wales, *Sociological Review* 40: 49 - 72.

BOYD, JAMES I. C. (1975), *The Festiniog Railway, Vol. 1 - History and Route 1800 - 1953*, Oakwood Press.

BRADLEY, TONY & LOWE, PHILIP (1984), Introduction: Locality, Rurality and Social Theory, in: Tony Bradley & Philip Lowe (eds.), *Locality and Rurality: Economy and Society in Rural Regions*, Geo Books, Norwich: 1 - 23.

BRODY, HUGH (1986), *Inishkillane — Change and Decline in the West of Ireland*, Faber & Faber, London.

BULMER, MARTIN (1985), The Rejuvenation of Community Studies? Neighbours, Networks and Policy, *Sociological Review* 33: 430 - 448.

CHAPMAN, C. G. (1971), *Milocca — A Sicilian Village*, Schenkman, Cambridge & London.

CHAPMAN, MALCOLM (1978), *The Gaelic Vision in Scottish Culture*, Croom Helm, London.

CHARSLEY, SIMON R. (1986), 'Glasgow's Miles Better': the Symbolism of Community and Identity in the City, in: Anthony P. Cohen (ed.), *Symbolising Boundaries — Identity and Diversity in British Cultures*, Anthropological Studies of Britain No. 2, Manchester University Press, Manchester: 171 - 186.

COHEN, ANTHONY P. (1978), Ethnographic Method in the Real Community, *Sociologia Ruralis* 18: 1 - 22.

COHEN, ANTHONY P. (1982a) (ed.), *Belonging — Identity and Social Organisation in British Rural Communities*, Anthropological Studies of Britain No. 1, Manchester University Press, Manchester.

COHEN, ANTHONY P. (1982b), Belonging: the Experience of Culture, in: Anthony P. Cohen (ed.), *Belonging—Identity and Social Organisation in British Rural Communities*, Anthropological Studies of Britain No. 1, Manchester University Press, Manchester: 1 - 17.

COHEN, ANTHONY P. (1982c), A Sense of Time, a Sense of Place: the Meaning of Close Social Association in Whalsay, Shetland, in: Anthony P. Cohen (ed.), *Belonging — Identity and Social Organisation in British Rural Communities*, Anthropological Studies of Britain No. 1, Manchester University Press, Manchester: 21 - 49.

COHEN, ANTHONY P. (1982d), Blockade: a Case Study of Local Consciousness in an Extra-Local Event, in: Anthony P. Cohen (ed.), *Belonging — Identity and Social Organisation in British Rural Communities*, Anthropological Studies of Britain No. 1, Manchester University Press, Manchester: 292 - 321.

COHEN, ANTHONY P. (1985a), *The Symbolic Construction of Community*, Ellis Horwood & Tavistock, London.

COHEN, ANTHONY P. (1985b), Symbolism and Social Change: Matters of Life and Death in Whalsay, Shetland, *Man N.S.* 20: 307 - 324.

COHEN, ANTHONY P. (1986a) (ed.), *Symbolising Boundaries — Identity and Diversity in British Cultures*, Anthropological Studies of Britain No. 2, Manchester University Press, Manchester.

COHEN, ANTHONY P. (1986b), Of Symbols and Boundaries, or, Does Ertie's Greatcoat Hold the Key?, in: Anthony P. Cohen (ed.), *Symbolising Boundaries — Identity and Diversity in British Cultures*, Anthropological Studies of Britain No. 2, Manchester University Press, Manchester: 1 -19.

COHEN, ANTHONY P. (1987), *Whalsay — Symbol, Segment and Boundary in a Shetland Island Community*, Anthropological Studies of Britain No. 3, Manchester University Press, Manchester.

COLE, J. W. (1977), Anthropology Comes Part-Way Home: Community Studies in Europe, *Annual Review of Anthropology* 6: 349 - 378.

DAVIES, ELWYN & REES, ALWYN D. (1960), *Welsh Rural Communities*, University of Wales Press, Cardiff.

DAVIS, J. (1977), *People of the Mediterranean — An Essay in Comparative Social Anthropology*, Routledge & Kegan Paul, London, Henley, and Boston.

DAY, GRAHAM (1986), The Sociology of Wales: Issues and Prospects, 1979 and 1985, in: Ian Hume & W. T. R. Pryce (eds.); *The Welsh and Their Country - Selected Readings in the Social Sciences*, Gomer Press, Llandysul, Dyfed: 153 - 175.

DAY, GRAHAM & FINTON, MARTIN (1975), Religion and Social Status in Rural Wales: Buchedd and its Lessons for Concepts of Stratification, *Sociological Review* 23: 867 - 891.

DAY, GRAHAM & MURDOCH, JONATHAN (1993), Locality and Community: Comming to Terms with Place, *Sociological Review* 41: 82 - 111.

DAY, GRAHAM & SUGGETT, RICHARD (1985), Conceptions of Wales and Welshness: Aspects of Nationalism in Nineteenth-Century Wales, in: J. Bujra & P. Littlewood & H. Newby & G. Rees & T. L. Rees (eds.), *Political Action and Social Identity — Class, Locality and Ideology*, Explorations in Sociology 19, British Sociological Association, Macmillan, London: 91 - 116.

DURKHEIM, EMILE ([1897]1966), *Suicide*, Glencoe, Illinois & London [first published as Le suicide, étude de sociologie, Paris 1897].

DURKHEIM, EMILE ([1893]1977), *Über die Teilung der sozialen Arbeit*, Suhrkamp, Frankfurt a. M. [first published as: De la division du travail social: étude sur l'organisation des societés supérieures, Paris 1893].

ELIAS, NORBERT (1974), Foreword — Towards a Theory of Communities, in: Colin Bell & Howard Newby (eds.), *The Sociology of the Community: a Selection of Readings*, Frank Cass, London: ix - xli.

EMMETT, ISABEL (1964), *A North Wales Village*, Routledge & Kegan Paul, London.

EMMETT, ISABEL (1978), Blaenau Boys in the Mid-1960s, in: Glyn Williams (ed.), *Social and Cultural Change in Contemporary Wales*, Routledge and Kegan Paul, London, Henley, Boston: 87 - 101.

EMMETT, ISABEL (1982a), Fe godwn ni eto: Stasis and Change in a Welsh Industrial Town, in: Anthony P. Cohen (ed.), *Belonging — Identity and Social Organisation in British Rural Communities*, Anthropological Studies of Britain No. 1, Manchester University Press, Manchester: 165 - 197.

EMMETT, ISABEL (1982b), Place, Community and Bilingualism in Blaenau Ffestiniog, in: Anthony P. Cohen (ed.), *Belonging — Identity and Social Organisation in British Rural Communities*, Anthropological Studies of Britain No. 1, Manchester University Press, Manchester: 202 - 221.

ENGELS, FRIEDRICH ([1884]1978), *Der Ursprung der Familie, des Privateigentums und des Staates — Im Anschluß an Lewis H. Morgans Forschungen*, Verlag Marxistische Blätter, Frankfurt a. M. [first published Zürich 1884]

ENNEW, JUDITH (1979), Self Image and Identity in the Hebrides, in: Anthony Jackson (ed.), *Way of Life and Identity*, North Sea Oil Panel Occasional Paper No. 4, Social Science Research Council, London: 49 - 62.

ENNEW, JUDITH (1980), *The Western Isles Today*, Cambridge University Press, Cambridge.

EVANS, ERIC J. (1983), *The Forging of the Modern State — Early Industrial Britain 1783-1870*, Longman, London and New York.

EVANS-PRITCHARD, E. (1962), *Essays in Social Anthropology*, Faber & Faber, London.

FORSYTHE, D. (1980), Urban Incomers and Rural Change: the Impact of Migrants from the City on Life in an Orkney Community, *Sociologia Ruralis* 20: 287 - 307.

FRANKENBERG, RONALD (1957), *Village on the Border — A Social Study of Religion, Politics and Football in a North Wales Community*, Cohen & West, London.
FRANKENBERG, RONALD (1966), British Community Studies: Problems of Synthesis, in: Michael Banton (ed.), *The Social Anthropology of Complex Societies*, ASA Monograph 4, Tavistock, London and New York: 123 - 154.
FRANKENBERG, RONALD (1969), *Communities in Britain — Social Life in Town and Country*, Penguin, Harmondsworth [2nd edn.].
FRANKENBERG, RONALD (1982), Introduction — A Social Anthropology for Britain?, in: Ronald Frankenberg (ed.), *Custom and Conflict in British Society*, Manchester University Press, Manchester: 1 - 35.
FRANKENBERG, RONALD (1986), Comment on: Marion McDonald, Celtic Ethnic Kinship and the Problem of Being English, *Current Anthropology* 27: 342.
FRANKENBERG, RONALD (1990), Village on the Border a Text Revisited 1989, in: Ronald Frankenberg, *Village on the Border - a Social Study of Religion, Politics and Football in a North Wales Community*, Waveland Press, Prospect Heights: 169 - 193 [reprint].
GEERTZ, CLIFFORD (1973), *The Interpretation of Cultures*, Basic Books, New York.
GIBBON, P. (1973), Arensberg and Kimball revisited, *Economy and Society* 2: 479 - 498.
GIDDENS, ANTHONY (1971), *Capitalism and Modern Social Theory*, Cambridge University Press, Cambridge.
GLUCKMAN, MAX (1963), *Order and Rebellion in Tribal Africa*, Cohen & West, London.
GLUCKMAN, MAX (1968), *Analysis of a Social Situation in Modern Zululand*, Rhodes-Livingstone Papers 28, Manchester University Press, Manchester [first published by the Rhodes-Livingston Institute, Northern Rhodesia 1958].
GREENWOOD, DAVYDD (1976), *Unrewarding Wealth — The Commercialization and Collapse of Agriculture in a Spanish Basque Town*, Cambridge University Press, Cambridge.
GRILLO, RALPH D. (1985), Applied Anthropology in the 1980s: Retrospect and Prospect, in: Ralph D. Grillo & Alan Rew (eds.), *Social Anthropology and Development Policy*, ASA Monograph 23, Tavistock, London and New York: 1 - 36.
GRILLO, RALPH D. (1989), *Dominant Languages — Language and Hierarchy in Britain and France*, Cambridge University Press, Cambridge.
GUSFIELD, JOSEPH R. (1975), *Community — A Critical Response*, Basil Blackwell, Oxford.
HAMILTON, PETER (1985), Editor's Foreword, in: Anthony P. Cohen, *The Symbolic Construction of Community*, Ellis Horwood & Tavistock, London: 7 - 9.
HECHTER, MICHAEL (1975), *Internal Colonialism — The Celtic Fringe in the British National Development 1536 - 1966*, Routledge & Kegan Paul, London.
HECHTER, MICHAEL (1985), Internal Colonialism Revisited, in: Edward A. Tiryakian & Ronald Rogowski (eds.), *New Nationalisms of the Developed West. Toward Explanation*, Allen & Unwin, Boston, London, Sydney: 17 - 26.
HEIBERG, MARIANNE (1989), *The Making of the Basque Nation*, Cambridge Studies in Social and Cultural Anthropology 66, Cambridge University Press, Cambridge.

HILLERY, G. A. Jr. (1955), Definitions of Community: Areas of Agreement, *Rural Sociology* 20: 111 - 123.

HUGHES, T. JONES (1960), Aberdaron — The Social Geography of a Small Region in the Llyn Peninsula, in: Elwyn Davies & Alwyn D. Rees (eds.), *Welsh Rural Communities*, University of Wales Press, Cardiff: 121 - 181.

HYMES, DELL (1974), The Use of Anthropology: Critical, Political, Personal, in: Dell Hymes (ed.), *Reinventing Anthropology*, Vintage Books, New York: 3 - 79.

JACKSON, ANTHONY (1987), Reflections on Ethnography at Home and the ASA, in: Anthony Jackson (ed.), *Anthropology at Home*, ASA Monograph 25, Tavistock, London and New York: 1 - 15.

JENKINS, DAVID (1960), Aberporth — A Study of a Coastal Village in South Cardiganshire, in: Elwyn Davies & Alwyn D. Rees (eds.), *Welsh Rural Communities*, University of Wales Press, Cardiff: 1 - 63.

JENKINS, DAVID (1980), Rural Society Inside Outside, in: David Smith (ed.), *A People and a Proletariat: Essays in the History of Wales 1780 - 1980*, Pluto Press & Llafur, Society for the Study of Welsh Labour History, London: 114 - 126.

JONES, EMRYS (1960), Tregaron — The Sociology of a Market Town in Central Cardiganshire, in: Elwyn Davies & Alwyn D. Rees (eds.), *Welsh Rural Communities*, University of Wales Press, Cardiff: 67 -117.

JONES, MERFYN (1980), Notes from the Margin: Class and Society in Nineteenth Century Gwynedd, in: David Smith (ed.), *A People and a Proletariat: Essays in the History of Wales 1780 - 1980*, Pluto Press & Llafur - Society for the Study of Welsh Labour History, London: 199 - 214.

KHLEIF, BUD B. (1978), Ethnic Awakening in the First World: the Case of Wales, in: Glyn Williams (ed.), *Social and Cultural Change in Contemporary Wales*, Routledge and Kegan Paul, London, Henley, Boston: 102 - 119.

KHLEIF, BUD B. (1980), *Language, Ethnicity, and Education in Wales*, Contributions to the Sociology of Language 28, Mouton Publishers, The Hague, Paris, New York.

KHLEIF, BUD B. (1984), Class, Ethnicity and Community in Wales: Issues and a Framework, *Journal of Ethnic Studies* 12: 1 - 16.

KUPER, ADAM (1987), *Anthropology and Anthropologists — The Modern British School*, Routledge & Kegan Paul, London and New York [revised edn.].

KUPER, ADAM (1988), *The Invention of Primitive Society — Transformations of an Illusion*, Routledge & Kegan Paul, London and New York.

LEACH, EDMUND (1977), *Custom, Law and Terrorist Violence*, Edinburgh University Press, Edinburgh.

LEACH, EDMUND (1986), *Social Anthropology*, Fontana Press, London [2nd impr.].

LEWIS, I. M. (1985), *Social Anthropology in Perspective — The Relevance of Social Anthropology*, Cambridge University Press, Cambridge [2nd edn.].

LOVERING, JOHN (1983), Uneven Development in Wales: the Changing Role of the British State, in: Glyn Williams (ed.), *Crisis of Economy and Ideology: Essays on Welsh Society*, S.S.R.C./B.S.A. Sociology of Wales Study Group, Bangor: 48 - 71.

MADGWICK, P. J. & GRIFFITHS, NON & WALKER, VALERIE (1973), *The Politics of Rural Wales - A Study of Cardiganshire*, Hutchinson, London.

MARX, KARL & ENGELS, FRIEDRICH ([1848]1971), The Communist Manifesto, in: Dirk J. Struik, *Birth of the Communist Manifesto — With Full Text of the Manifesto, all Prefaces by Marx and Engels, Early Drafts by Engels and Other Supplementary Material*, International Publishers, New York [first published as: Manifest der Kommunistischen Partei, London 1848].

MCFARLANE, GRAHAM (1986), 'It's not as simple as that': the Expression of Catholic and Protestant Boundary in Northern Irish Rural Communities, in: Anthony P. Cohen (ed.), *Symbolising Boundaries — Identity and Diversity in British Cultures*, Anthropological Studies of Britain No. 2, Manchester University Press, Manchester: 88 - 104.

MEWETT, PETER G. (1982a), Associational Categories and the Social Location of Relationships in a Lewis Crofting Community, in: Anthony P. Cohen (ed.), *Belonging — Identity and Social Organisation in British Rural Communities*, Anthropological Studies of Britain No. 1, Manchester University Press, Manchester: 101 - 130.

MEWETT, PETER G. (1982b), Exiles, Nicknames, Social Identities and the Production of Local Consciousness in a Lewis Crofting Community, in: Anthony P. Cohen (ed.), *Belonging — Identity and Social Organisation in British Rural Communities*, Anthropological Studies of Britain No. 1, Manchester University Press, Manchester: 222 - 246.

MEWETT, PETER G. (1983), Economic Brokerage and Peripheral Underdevelopment in the Isle of Lewis, *Sociological Review* 31: 427 - 452.

MEWETT, PETER G. (1986), Boundaries and Discourse in a Lewis Crofting Community, in: Anthony P. Cohen (ed.), *Symbolising Boundaries — Identity and Diversity in British Cultures*, Anthropological Studies of Britain No. 2, Manchester University Press, Manchester: 71 - 87.

MEWETT, PETER G. (1988), Setting and Situation in Migration from the Isle of Lewis, *Ethnos* 53: 204 - 227.

MICHAEL, DAI (1983), Before Alwyn: Early Social Thought, Action and Research in Wales, in: Glyn Williams (ed.), *Crisis of Economy and Ideology: Essays on Welsh Society*, S.S.R.C./B.S.A. Sociology of Wales Study Group, Bangor: 17 - 34.

MINCHINTON, W. E. & STACEY, MARGARET & PLOWMAN, D. E. G. (1962), Local Social Status in England and Wales, *Sociological Review* 10: 161 - 202.

MORGAN, KENNETH O. (1971), Welsh Nationalism: the Historical Background, *Journal of Contemporary History* 6: 153 - 172.

MORGAN, KENNETH O. (1982), *Rebirth of a Nation: Wales 1880-1980*, Oxford University Press, Oxford.

NADEL-KLEIN, JANE (1991), Reweaving the Fringe: Localism, Tradition, and Representation in British Ethnography, *American Ethnologist* 18: 500 - 517.

NAIRN, TOM (1981), *The Break-Up of Britain: Crisis and Neo-Nationalism*, New Left Books, London.

NEWBY, HOWARD (1979), *Green and pleasant Land? – Social change in rural England*, Hutchinson, London.

OSMOND, JOHN (1978), *Creative Conflict - The Politics of Welsh Devolution*, Gomer Press, Llandysul, Dyfed/Routledge & Kegan Paul, London.

OWEN, TREFOR M. (1960), Chapel and Community in Glan Llyn, Merioneth, in: Elwyn Davies & Alwyn D. Rees (eds.), *Welsh Rural Communities*, University of Wales Press, Cardiff: 185 - 248.

OWEN, TREFOR M. (1986), Community Studies in Wales: An Overview, in: Ian Hume & W.T.R. Pryce (eds.); *The Welsh and Their Country - Selected Readings in the Social Sciences*, Gomer Press, Llandysul: 91 - 133.

PETERS, E. LLOYD (1972), Aspects of the Control of Moral Ambiguities: A Comparative Analysis of Two Culturally Disparate Modes of Social Control, in: Max Gluckman (ed.), *The Allocation of Responsibility*, Manchester University Press, Manchester: 109 - 162.

PITT-RIVERS, J. A. (1954), *The People of the Sierra*, Weidenfeld & Nicolson, London.

RADCLIFFE-BROWN, A. R. (1952), *Structure and Function in Primitive Society*, Cohen & West, London.

REDFIELD, ROBERT (1947), The Folk Society, *American Journal of Sociology* 52: 293 - 308.

REDFIELD, ROBERT (1955), *The Little Community — Viewpoints for the Study of a Human Whole*, The Gottesman Lectures Uppsala University 1955, Almquist & Wiksells, Uppsala and Stockholm.

REES, ALWYN D. (1950), *Life in a Welsh Countryside — A Social Study of Llanfihangel yng Ngwynfa*, University of Wales Press, Cardiff.

REES, ALWYN D. (1978), A Nation With a Split Personality, *Planet* 42 (April): 11 - 13.

REES, GARETH (1985), Introduction: Class, Locality and Ideology, in: J. Bujra & P. Littlewood & H. Newby & G. Rees & T. L. Rees (eds.), *Political Action and Social Identity — Class, Locality and Ideology*, Explorations in Sociology 19, British Sociological Association, Macmillan, London: 1 - 15.

RICHARDS, AUDREY (1981), Foreword, in: Marilyn Strathern, *Kinship at the Core. An Anthropology of Elmdon, a Village in North-West Essex in the Nineteen-Sixties*, Cambridge University Press, Cambridge: xi - xxvi.

ROBBINS, KEITH (1985), From Imperial Power to European Partner 1901-1975 — Overview, in: Christopher Haigh (ed.), *The Cambridge Historical Encyclopedia of Great Britain and Ireland*, Guild Publishing, London: 290 - 292.

ROBIN, JEAN (1980), *Elmdon: Continuity and Change in a North-West Essex Village, 1861 - 1964*, Cambridge University Press, Cambridge.

SAGER, PETER (1985), *Wales — Literatur und Politik, Industrie und Landschaft*, DuMont, Köln.
SANDERS, I. (1949), *Balkan Village*, University of Kentucky Press, Lexington.
SIMPSON, RICHARD L. (1974), Sociology of the Community: Current Status and Prospects, in: Colin Bell & Howard Newby (eds.), *The Sociology of the Community: a Selection of Readings*, Frank Cass and Co. Ltd., London: 312 - 334.
SMITH, ANTHONY D. (1991), National Identity, Penguin, Harmondsworth.
SMITH, DAVID (1980), Wales Through the Looking-Glass, in: David Smith (ed.), *A People and a Proletariat: Essays in the History of Wales 1780 - 1980*, Pluto Press & Llafur, Society for the Study of Welsh Labour History, London: 215 - 239.
SOUTHALL, AIDAN (1959), An Operational Theory of Role, *Human Relations* 12: 17 - 34.
SOUTHALL, AIDAN (1973), The Density of Role-Relationships as a Universal Index of Urbanization, in: Aidan Southall (ed.), *Urban Anthropology — Cross Cultural Studies of Urbanization*, Oxford University Press, New York, London, Toronto: 71 - 106.
STACEY, MARGARET (1974), The Myth of Community Studies, in: Colin Bell & Howard Newby (eds.), *The Sociology of the Community: a Selection of Readings*, Frank Cass and Co. Ltd., London: 13 - 26.
STRATHERN, MARILYN (1981), *Kinship at the Core. An Anthropology of Elmdon, a Village in North-West Essex in the Nineteen-Sixties*, Cambridge University Press, Cambridge.
STRATHERN, MARILYN (1982a), The Place of Kinship: Kin, Class and Village Status in Elmdon, Essex, in: Anthony P. Cohen (ed.), *Belonging — Identity and Social Organisation in British Rural Communities*, Anthropological Studies of Britain No. 1, Manchester University Press, Manchester: 72 - 100.
STRATHERN, MARILYN (1982b), The Village as an Idea: Constructs of Village-ness in Elmdon, Essex, in: Anthony P. Cohen (ed.), *Belonging — Identity and Social Organisation in British Rural Communities*, Anthropological Studies of Britain No. 1, Manchester University Press, Manchester: 247 - 277.
STRATHERN, MARILYN (1984), Localism Displaced: a 'Vanishing Village' in Rural England, *Ethnos* 49: 43 - 61.
STRATHERN, MARILYN (1987), The Limits of Auto-Anthropology, in: Anthony Jackson (ed.), *Anthropology at Home*, ASA Monograph 25, Tavistock, London and New York: 16 - 37.
SYMES, DAVID G. (1981), Rural Community Studies in Great Britain, in: Jean-Louis Durand-Drouhin & Lili-Maria Szwengrub (eds.), *Rural Community Studies in Europe — Trends, Selected and Annotated Bibliographies, Analyses, Volume 1*, European Coordination Centre for Research and Documentation in Social Sciences, Pergamon, Oxford: 17 - 67.
TÖNNIES, FERDINAND ([1887]1979), *Gemeinschaft und Gesellschaft*, Wissenschaftliche Buchgesellschaft, Darmstadt [first published 1887].

TURNER, VICTOR W. (1957), *Schism and Continuity in an African Society — A Study of Ndembu Villiage Life*, Manchester University Press, Manchester.

URWIN, DEREK W. (1982), Territorial Structures and Political Developments in the United Kingdom, in: Stein Rokkan & Derek W. Urwin (eds.), *The Politics of Territorial Identity - Studies in European Regionalism*, Sage, London: 19 - 73.

WENGER, G. CLARE (1980), *Mid Wales: Deprivation or Development*, Board of Celtic Studies, Social Science Monographs 5, University of Wales Press, Cardiff.

WILLIAMS, COLIN H. (1984), Ideology and the Interpretation of Minority Cultures, *Political Geography Quarterly* 3: 105 - 125.

WILLIAMS, GLANMOR (1979), *Religion, Language, and Nationality in Wales*, University of Wales Press, Cardiff.

WILLIAMS, GLYN (1978), Introduction, in: Glyn Williams (ed.), *Social and Cultural Change in Contemporary Wales*, Routledge and Kegan Paul, London, Henley, Boston: 1 - 15.

WILLIAMS, GLYN (1980), Industrialisation, Inequality, and Deprivation in Rural Wales, in: Gareth Rees & Teresa L. Rees (eds.), *Poverty and Social Inequality in Wales*, Croom Helm, London: 168 - 184.

WILLIAMS, GLYN (1983), On Class and Status Groups in Welsh Rural Society, in: Glyn Williams (ed.), *Crisis of Economy and Ideology: Essays on Welsh Society*, S.S.R.C./B.S.A. Sociology of Wales Study Group, Bangor: 134 - 146.

WILLIAMS, GLYN (1986), Recent Trends in the Sociology of Wales, in: Ian Hume & W. T. R. Pryce (eds.); *The Welsh and Their Country - Selected Readings in the Social Sciences*, Gomer Press, Llandysul, Dyfed: 176 - 192.

WILLIAMS, GWYN A. (1991), *When was Wales? — A History of the Welsh*, Penguin, Harmondsworth.

WILLIAMS, W. M. (1956), *The Sociology of an English Village: Gosforth*, Routledge & Kegan Paul, London.

WILLIAMS, W. M. (1963), *A West Country Village Ashworthy — Family, Kinship, and Land*, Routledge & Kegan Paul, London.

INDEX

A

Anderson, Benedict 146
Ardener, Edwin 70-72
Arensberg, Conrad M. 27, 89
Arensberg, Conrad M. & Kimball, Solon T. 9, 12–15, 43, 45, 90, 107–109
Aull Davies, Charlotte 78

B

Barnes, J. A. 18, 21
Barth, Fredrik 9, 46
Bell, Colin & Newby, Howard 7, 13, 16, 18, 28, 29, 32-33, 38, 66
Bierstadt, Robert 33
Bloch, Maurice 11 (fn.), 23
Boissevain, Jeremy 57, 59, 60
Boon, James A. 7, 47
Borland, John 145–148
Bottt, Elisabeth 21
Boyd, James I. C. 132
Bradley, Tony 39
Brody, Hugh 107–109

C

Chapman, C. G. 27
Chapman, Malcolm 65
Charsley, Simon R. 29
Cherry, Colin 20
Cohen, Anthony P. 10, 29-31, 35-39, 42–55, 56 (fn.), 59, 65, 69 (fn.), 72, 87–88, 119, 123, 146, 152
Cole, J. W. 27, 37 (fn.)

D

Darwin, Charles 5-6
Davies, Elwyn 74, 89, 97, 110, 116, 119
Davis, J. 27
Day, Graham 29 (fn.), 58–59, 74, 76, 79, 82, 83, 88, 111–115, 140–145
Denney, David 145–148
Dodd, A. H. 120
Durkheim, Emile 6, 7, 8, 10, 11 (fn.), 15, 24, 25, 27, 30, 44, 96

E

Elias, Norbert 7
Elis-Thomas, Dafydd 147
Emmett, Isabel 37, 63, 109, 116, 119, 126–132, 144, 157-158
Engels, Friedrich 6
Ennew, Judith 30, 37 (fn.)
Evans, Eric J. 5
Evans, Ifor L. 89
Evans-Pritchard, E. 33 (fn.)

F

Fevre, Ralph 145–148
Fitton, Martin 111–115
Forde, Daryll 89
Forsythe, Diana 65
Frankenberg, Ronald 9, 18–26, 29-32, 40, 110, 116-125, 129, 139, 140, 159

G

Geertz, Clifford 45
Gibbon, P. 107–109
Giddens, Anthony 24-26
Gluckman, Max 18, 23-24, 116-117, 120, 122 (fn.)
Goffman, Erving. 20
Greenwood, Davydd 108–109
Griffiths, Non 158
Grillo, Ralph D. 57, 59, 76, 82
Gusfield, Joseph R. 6-8, 26, 30-31

H

Hamilton, Peter 28
Hechter, Michael 5, 40, 74–76
Heiberg, Marianne 79
Hillery, G. A. Jr. 29
Hughes, T. Jones 97–98
Hymes, Dell 69 (fn.)

J

Jackson, Anthony 8, 28, 30-35, 37, 42
Jenkins, David 97, 103–107, 108, 110–115, 119, 129, 135
Jones, Emrys 97, 99–100, 108, 112, 113 (fn.)
Jones, Merfyn 77, 133
Jones, Tudur 147 (fn.)

K

Khleif, Bud B. 63, 84–85, 136, 144, 155 (fn.), 157
Kimball, Solon T. *see Arensberg & Kimball*
Kuper, Adam 6 (fn.), 18, 28, 35, 42

L

Leach, Edmund 11, 28, 33, 36, 44, 59
Lewis I. M. 11
Lewis, Saunders 81
Lovering, John 77
Lowe Philip 39

M

Madgwick, P. J. 158
Malinowski, Bronislaw 11, 12
Mao Tse-Tung 120
Marx, Karl 6-7, 23-24, 26-27, 120
McFarlane, Graham 35
Merton, R. K. 24 (fn.)
Mewett Peter G. 37 (fn.), 64–65, 108
Michael, Dai 109
Minchinton, W. E. 110
Mitchell, J. C. 18
Morgan, Kenneth O. 77, 80-82, 87, 133, 149
Murdoch 29 (fn.), 58–59, 140–143

N

Nadel-Klein, Jane 57–61, 63–65
Nairn, Tom 5, 76-78
Newby, Howard 142, 143 *see also Bell & Newby*

O

Osmond, John 82, 86
Owen, Trefor M. 18, 32, 33, 97, 100-103, 105-106, 117, 140

P

Peters, Emrys Lloyd 92–93, 118, 154
Pitt-Rivers, J. A. 79
Plowman D. E. G. 110

R

Radcliffe-Brown, A. R. 11-12
Redfield, Robert 9, 15–17
Rees, Alwyn D. 12 (fn.), 30, 74, 89-98, 107, 109, 110, 112, 116, 119, 141, 159
Rees, Gareth 39
Richards, Audrey 36, 37, 66
Robbins, Keith 38
Robin, Jean 36
Rose, David 29, 38

S

Sager, Peter 86, 133

Sanders, I. 27
Saunders, Peter 29, 38
Simpson, Richard L. 12, 16
Smith, Anthony D. 84, 144
Smith, David 78
Southall, Aidan 22
Spencer, Herbert 6
Stacey, Margaret 11, 110, 141
Strathern, Marilyn 35-37, 58, 61-63, 66–70, 72
Suggett, Richard 144–145
Symes David G. 31

T

Thomas, R. S. 86
Tönnies, Ferdinand 6-8, 10, 15, 27, 30, 96, 146, 149
Turner, V. W. 54, 120

U

Urwin, Derek W. 40

W

Walker, Valerie 158
Wallman, Sandra 59
Weber, Max 23
Wenger, Clare C. 150
Williams, Colin H. 80 (fn.), 155
Williams, Glanmor 150
Williams, Glyn 74, 80, 83-84, 89, 109, 112, 114-115, 132, 139-140, 149, 155
Williams, Gwyn A. 78, 79, 139 (fn.)
Williams, Raymond 146
Williams, W. M. 89 (fn.)